The Abingdon Women's Preaching Annual

Series 2
Year C

Compiled and Edited by
Leonora Tubbs Tisdale

Abingdon Press
Nashville

THE ABINGDON WOMEN'S PREACHING ANNUAL

Copyright © 2000 by Abingdon Press

This book is printed on recycled, acid-free, elemental-chlorine–free paper.

ISBN 0-687-08193-9
ISSN 1086-8240

00 01 02 03 04 05 06 07 08 09 — 10 9 8 7 6 5 4 3 2 1

MANUFACTURED IN THE UNITED STATES OF AMERICA

In Loving Memory

of My Two Grandmothers,

Sarah Hansell Cousar and Ruth Rennie Tubbs,

Who Modeled for Me

Two Very Different Ways

of Being Faithful Women of the Word

Contents

Introduction

One of my favorite images of the preacher is one that Barbara Brown Taylor explores in her book *The Preaching Life*. The preacher, says Taylor, is a "detective of divinity" who goes out into the world, looking for God under every rock and twig. When she has glimpsed signs of God's extraordinary presence in the midst of the mundane (a God she is enabled to recognize through the lens of the Scriptures), she then goes into the pulpit while she is still shaking and trembling with the wonder of the discovery, offering to share that treasure she has found with others.[1]

In this volume of sermons and worship resources, a number of detectives of divinity (sixteen, to be exact) offer to share their discoveries with you. Ordinary pastors and chaplains, students and teachers, partners and friends, mothers and grandmothers, these women first reflect on the assigned lectionary texts for the Sundays and feast days of the Christian year, and then go into the world to see where they glimpse signs of a God like the one they encountered in the Scriptures. As they do so, they not only name God in the world, they also rename theology from the standpoint of their experience as women in the world.

Sylvia Guinn-Ammons, encountering Mary's Advent Song through the lens of Third World liberation theology, has her eyes opened anew to the radical nature of that song "staccatoed by the kicking of tiny feet," and urges us, like Mary, to have courage to "sing of the unborn dreams kicking within us waiting to be born." Ella Pearson Mitchell, recognizing our absorption at Christmastime with material gift-giving, invites us to present the Christ Child instead with a "basket of the fruits of righteousness" and provides some very down-to-earth suggestions for how we and our families might do so.

Janet Schlichting, O.P., long acquainted with Lent as the season of "giving up," encourages us on Ash Wednesday to re-vision Lent as a time of "befriending"—"our soul, our body, our neighbor, our world and by all of this, dwelling in God's befriending." Calling us to embrace both the Hole in our lives (that within us which is needy and incomplete) and the Whole (Body of Christ and human community), this detective of divinity invites us to embrace those classic Christian disciplines—prayer, fasting and almsgiving—not as unwanted guests to be endured for a season, but as welcome and welcoming friends. Meanwhile, Laura Loving reminds us that Lent is also a time for telling the stories of our faith. When we, like Jesus during his temptations, are "teetering on the turret in the wilderness," we too can find that by recounting the stories of faith and the faithful, we are borne up like angels.

When the Easter season rolls around, Karen Pidcock-Lester reminds us that resurrection is not something that happens once in our lives. Rather we disciples of the risen Christ are meant to keep on "practicing resurrection" our whole lives through, hoeing and planting its seeds in whatever soil we find ourselves, without undue concern for the results (which are always up to God). And on Pentecost Day Mary Kraus invokes the image of medieval cathedrals, which had literal "Holy Spirit holes" in their ceilings through which doves and flames of fire were released on Pentecost Day, in order to invite us to open up the spaces in our own lives through which fresh inbreakings of the Spirit can occur.

These detectives of divinity use fresh images and language to help us see God in unexpected ways and places, and by sharing their own insightful discoveries with us, help us believe we might unearth such treasures, too—even when looking through the lens of texts that have become so familiar that we expect to see nothing new through them at all.

So sit back, watch, and listen. For the pulpit is about to be strewn with all sorts of treasures—some still covered with twigs and mud and debris. And if you look closely, you might just glimpse something (someone?) Holy in the midst of it all.

Leonora Tubbs Tisdale
Summer (Ordinary Time) 1999
Princeton Theological Seminary
Princeton, New Jersey

1. Barbara Brown Taylor, *The Preaching Life* (Boston: Cowley, 1993), pp. 15, 81.

First Sunday of Advent

Susan Henry-Crowe

Jeremiah 33:14-16: The reign of God comes not only beyond time and this world, but also in history, in the present time, and in the world that is yet to be.

Psalm 25:1-10: The plea of God to be remembered is the focal point of the Psalm. "Remember me," God says, as we watch, wait, and wonder.

1 Thessalonians 3:9-13: Paul's words enable the church to think about Christ's coming in both an existential and an eschatological sense.

Luke 21:25-36: For those who know Christ, the final shaking of heaven and earth will not be an occasion for fear and distress. The day of judgment is the day of grace. Prayerful watching and freedom from indulgence and anxiety are foci for Advent.

REFLECTIONS

The eschatology of Advent is the focus of the readings. The day of judgment and the day of grace are one and the same. The hymn says it well, "Earth has no sorrow that heaven cannot heal."[1] In Advent, our posture and our attitude in prayer must be of watchfulness and wonder. In all the experiences of life, it is as we watch and discover the wonder, that God's presence is made known to us.

A SERMON BRIEF
(based on Luke 21:25-36)

This is the beginning of a new age, the new millennium. We have weathered apocalyptic predictions of signs of the end time. After

11

twenty centuries, wars, poverty, and injustice still reign. The world is racked with violence, yet not destroyed. It is filled with destruction, yet not overcome. We live amidst injustice, poverty, and prejudice, yet still there are signs of justice, fullness, and hope. And we watch. And we wait. And we wonder.

Recently I was driving a long and boring (that is, not full of distractions) section of Interstate 20 between South Carolina and Georgia. It is a stretch of road that symbolizes movement from the past to the present. It denotes movement from one home to another, one season to the next, one world to another. It literally is the road from my former life to my present life. I found myself carefully watching the rearview mirror as I drove, looking back on where I had been.

The year had been monumentally eventful. My only child, my woman child, had graduated from college. My mother, having lived every day of her eighty-three and a half years, had died on the second Sunday of Advent. She was now free from years of living with sickeningly chronic blood diseases, probably contracted from her life's work as a nurse anesthetist. A year had passed since my child's graduation and six months since my mother's untimely, timely death.

Grief was taking hold of my body. I was tired. Some nights were sleepless. Restlessness marked many days. An ordinary experience could touch deep sadness. The past few weeks had marked several anniversaries: Mother's Day, leaving me motherless; her May birthday; the anniversary of my sister's tragic death some twenty-five years ago. My rich life as a pastor to a university community was all too often filled with experiences of death and grief. Absence created sorrow which was difficult to bear. There was little in which I found great comfort. Friends, food, busyness, sleep, gardening—all stirred memories which, in this season, felt like too much absence and emptiness.

Looking into the rearview mirror called me to the former things, the former days. Life as a child. Life as a mother. Life in ministry. Life in a full and yet finally failed marriage. Looking back stirred reminders of tragedy, death, sorrow. And looking back stirred reminders of love, life, parties, celebrations, joys, and creativity. Looking back conjured up memories which served as reminders of what would never again be and grief which was being transformed into something new and different.

Driving along this boring road uncluttered by distractions, I found myself watching the road ahead. I knew that my child's graduation and my mother's death had opened the future in ways I could not yet articulate and would only appreciate as I lived into it. The future was

12

ahead and I could not see it. *But* there were plans beginning to be formed. There would be a trip with my dear friend to Germany, which one year before I could not have made. There was a love relationship, turning into a commitment to living life together. Not even being fifty years old, there was a strong possibility that there would be yet two or more decades of life to live.

Driving into Atlanta I knew the future lay ahead, but it was yet to come into its own. There would be surprises, challenges, hopes, dreams, friends, communities, some disappointments, and heartaches.

Advent is God's coming into what has been, what is, and what is yet to be. Advent is God's activity and God's way of entering human history. As death came in Advent, so did life. As sorrow came in Advent, so did freedom. As grief came in Advent, so did possibility.

God's redemption is of such magnanimity, such kindness, such generosity, such compassion that the whole earth and all that is therein reverberates with signs. God comes to redeem the present moment. God comes to hold all that is to be.

The day of judgment is the day of driving from the former days into the season that is yet to be. It is the journey of judgment in which sin, sickness, sorrow are redeemed, and which becomes the journey of grace.

We watch. We wait. We wonder.

SUGGESTIONS FOR WORSHIP

Call to Worship[2]

LEADER: The day foretold is coming.
PEOPLE: When our tired eyes will behold a fire, a blazing star in the eastern sky!
LEADER: The one foretold is coming.
PEOPLE: Whose light will shine through the deepest gloom.
LEADER: The day is at hand!
PEOPLE: Your redemption is drawing near!

Prayer

We are watching, Redeeming God. In all times, in all places, we watch for a sign that your Redeeming One is drawing near. We keep

13

the vigil for ourselves and for the earth, for we desire to know the time for your visitation. Only the Redeeming One can ease the load and make our burdens light. Only the Redeeming One can transform our poverty of spirit into abundance. Only the Redeeming One can restore our neglect of truth into a commitment to justice. We wait. We watch. We wonder. Amen.

Benediction

Hold us in our waiting, for you will surely come.
Keep us in our watching, for you will not be long.
Fill us in our wonder, for your redemption will bring us joy!
Amen.

1. Thomas Moore, "Come, Ye Disconsolate" in *The United Methodist Hymnal* (Nashville: The United Methodist Publishing House, 1995), p. 510.
2. Adapted from Phyllis Cole and Everett Tilson, *Litanies and Other Prayers for the Revised Common Lectionary, Year C* (Nashville: Abingdon Press, 1994), p. 15.

Second Sunday of Advent

Ella Pearson Mitchell

Malachi 3:1-4: The Prophet Malachi foretells a forerunning special messenger of God's judgment, as in Isaiah 40:3, and then wonders who can stand when this messenger appears.

Luke 1:68-79: The elderly priest Zachariah sings a song rejoicing that his son John will be the forerunner of God's messenger, who will bring salvation and guide our feet in the way of peace.

Luke 3:1-6: Zachariah's prediction of a Savior is continued in the proclamation of John, his son, using Isaiah's prophetic language that "all flesh shall see the salvation of God" (Isaiah 40:3-5).

Philippians 1:3-11: The apostle Paul greets his beloved church at Philippi with a prayer of thankfulness and the desire that the work begun in them by the living Christ might be fulfilled with even greater fruits of righteousness.

REFLECTIONS

I am deeply committed to the principle that every sermon should have, in addition to its biblical enlightenment, a basically behavioral purpose, or bottom line. The ultimate goal is not factual, data-oriented or cognitive. Rather, the goal is to move hearers to live out the Word after it is understood—to transform attitudes and/or actions in the direction of the new person in Christ Jesus as model and empowerer. As I view it, the first three passages above were quoted in the early church with a primary goal of validating Jesus as the One sent according to God's prior plan. Luke and others had a behavioral purpose of winning the acceptance of Jesus in a world in which he was still mostly unheard of. In our time and culture, with crosses on steeples everywhere and Christmas and Easter as major public holidays, such an acceptance can hardly be thought of as a critically important goal. It has already been widely attained. The challenges of our time lie in the area of the kingdom purposes for which Jesus came. In the light of this perspective, Paul's word to the Philippians offers a very practical suggestion for the observance of Advent and the choice of a "Christmas present" for Jesus. It's *his* birthday, not ours.

Our sermon text, then, found in verse 11, speaks of "Being filled with the fruits of righteousness, which are by Jesus Christ [and are already begun, v. 6], unto the glory and praise of God" (KJV). While we adore the Christ Child, in awe and wonder at the Incarnation, God with us, we are bound to have a deep desire to give. It has always been thus; only in recent decades has commercialization become so overwhelming. This inclusion of the Philippians passage in the lectionary readings is a way of suggesting that we bring to the Christmas rite, at the side of the manger, a basket of the fruits of righteousness. Without such a gift, all other observance of Christmas is hollow anyway. There is no better time for recommitment than this season of warm, tender hearts and awe and wonder.

A SERMON BRIEF
"What to Give the Baby"

This is the Christmas shopping season, as everybody knows. Do I dare to be really nosy and ask you if Jesus is on your list for presents? It's *his* birthday, you know. And may I meddle further and suggest not only that you add his name, but that you place it at the top of the list? This, of course, raises major questions for serious shoppers. Just what is this preacher getting at?

Well, I'd like to offer some helpful suggestions. In the first place, most Christmas gifts are bought with money. We are jostled about in the frantic shopping crowds in order that we may lay down money for gifts, some useful and some just part of the tradition. The present says to the receiver, "This is what I felt I could afford." And many people of limited means are deeply depressed at Christmas because they don't have the money it takes to say what they want to say.

Some sensitive people in our time have taken to *making* presents with their own hands. It conveys a warmer personal message. Even if it isn't any more useful than many bought presents, a handcrafted gift shows how much of the real you, as opposed to your hard money, is in the gift. But even this requires some shopping, if just for materials and wrappings.

The apostle Paul offers an idea that would work at Christmas in a most appropriate way. You don't have to shop for it, and it is very warmly personal. In fact, it comes from within the giver—from the very depths of a person. Paul reminds the Philippians that God "has begun a good work in you" (1:6) and urges them to be "filled with the fruits of righteousness, which are by Jesus Christ, unto the glory and praise of God" (1:11 KJV). In other words, each of us has the option of pleasing our Lord on his birthday, just by seriously rededicating ourselves to continuing the work Christ has already begun in us. That work is evident in the fruits of righteousness which we live out.

People think of self-denial and spiritual discipline during Lent, but Christmas is no less a time for renewal. Indeed, the Christmas basket of the "fruits of righteousness," which Paul suggests, may very well require a wider scope of altered lifestyle. But this plan has the advantage of the positive motivation of a lovingly reordered life, offered to him as Holy Infant, who in maturity has already given us the empowerment by beginning this "good work" within us.

Paul's plan contrasts further with the all too common shopping pattern in that the latter diminishes the donor's resources. Many people mortgage a year's salary with credit purchases made for the obligatory exchange of gifts, with or without love. Others suffer through Christmas, in sorrow over their inability to lavish on their loved ones the gifts they themselves longed for as children.

Still others come to Christmas Day exhausted from the effort of observing it in the manner of our commercially influenced culture. They may have the money, but they are physically and emotionally exhausted by the effort required. I am reminded of our four children who for years gave only to Jesus at Christmas. In their early teens they voted to conform to this "world," just to see what it was like. A "large" sum of two hundred dollars was appropriated, and small teams chose and purchased gifts for each of us. They had hardly completed one shopping expedition when they wanted out. Their frustration lay in the high prices paid for thoughtful choices that proved useless. Never again did they vote to conform to the cultural context, and they gladly received their many gifts on their own birthdays.

Paul's plan for concentrating on a basket of the fruits of righteousness for the Baby Jesus has the marvelous advantage of enhancing the givers, not depleting them. Those who rededicate their lives at

Christmas achieve the subtle side effect of abundant life for their "trouble" all during the ensuing year. That doesn't mean that no money is spent, but it does mean that the gifts are for Jesus, not us and our friends. Our family delighted in breeder rabbits for Ecuador, and, in later years, a gift to the Southern Christian Leadership Conference. The contents of Jesus' Christmas basket are influenced by Jesus' own advice that those who live for self lose real life, and those who lose their lives for his sake will find life abundant (Luke 9:24; John 10:10*b*).

The bottom line, however, is that the gifts in the basket of righteousness not only bless the giver but have implications for the whole world. That stable boy at Bethlehem took part in the plan of salvation for the world. When, from within, Mary gave birth to that baby, her earlier song of praise was more justified than she dreamed: "From now on, all the succeeding generations will say that I was blessed to be able to give this birth" (Luke 1:48*b*, paraphrase).

Whatever other gifts accompany our fruits of righteousness, and whatever they cost or don't cost, I can say after sixty years of trying to fill the basket that there is no greater joy and no greater fulfillment. A haunting Christmas carol from late-nineteenth-century England has a poor child summing it up by asking:

> What can I give him, Poor as I am?
> If I were a shepherd, I would bring a lamb;
> If I were a wise man, I would do my part;
> Yet what I can I give him: Give my heart.
> (Christina G. Rossetti, 1876)

SUGGESTIONS FOR WORSHIP

Call to Worship

LEADER: Listen: God will send the messenger to prepare the way.
PEOPLE: **Who is the One who will come after?**
ALL: **The messenger of God's promises, to bring us great peace and joy!**

Prayers of the People

Almighty and ever present God, we praise and honor you this day. As John the Baptist sought to herald the bringer of salvation, inspire us to continue with love and loyalty to lift up Jesus Christ. We bless you for the invitation to a creative new adventure that can make the world a better place. We pray for strength and courage to alter the traditions that hold us so tightly. As we join in Paul's prayer that echoes down the centuries, lead us and guide us. "And this I pray, that your love may abound yet more and more in knowledge and in all judgment; That ye may approve things that are excellent; that ye may be sincere and without offense till the day of Christ; Being filled with the fruits of righteousness, which are by Jesus Christ, unto the glory and praise of God" (Philippians 1:9-11 KJV). Amen.

Benediction

Depart from this hallowed place to bear the fruits of righteousness. And the peace that passeth all understanding be yours, through Jesus Christ, to whom be glory, honor, and praise forever and evermore! Amen.

Third Sunday of Advent

Ella Pearson Mitchell

Zephaniah 3:14-20: After lengthy proclamations of severe judgment, Zephaniah sings a song of prophetic hope to Israel, that her punishment and disgrace are over, that God will be in her midst.

Isaiah 12:2-6: In remembrance of both his judgmental prophecies (chapters 5, 9, and 10) and his hopeful vision (10:27*d*-32), the prophet raises on behalf of Israel a song of praise and renewed faithfulness and hope in God.

Luke 3:7-18: John the Baptist declares God's judgment with such power that not only ordinary citizens, but also priests and soldiers, are moved to ask how they can be saved. John answers with a call to repentance and the announcement of the coming of another, not himself, as Messiah.

Philippians 4:4-7: Paul's letter of deep spiritual affection to the church at Philippi is compelled to deal with a division between two sisters; this passage might be summed up as suggesting, as a solution, that mouths filled with prayer and praise have no room left for fussing.

REFLECTIONS

It amazes me that in the most favored of his planted churches there should be what Paul tactfully refers to as Euodias and Syntyche not being of the same mind. Who are these quarreling saints who have labored so faithfully and side by side with Paul? I am compelled to think that one of them, possibly Euodias, is the same person to whom Luke refers as Lydia (Acts 16:14). There is no other way to explan why Paul's dye-selling hostess is not mentioned in this letter.

And it is easy to surmise that Luke only remembered her Lydian origin (Thyatira) and called her by that name. This would explain why the help of a female pillar of the church like "Lydia" was not enlisted along with that of a presumably male "true yokefellow" (thought by some scholars to be an individual and by some to be the church as a whole) (v. 3).

Thus arises the issue of how the first European convert, a woman of means and of great hospitality, could stoop to quarrel. Her most humble invitation to Paul hardly suggests power-hungry arrogance. As I empathize my way into the dynamics, they must have something to do with new and inexperienced Christian women in the cultural rarity of being in power for the first time. As the apostles labored among the women, the women had yet to learn how to handle authority between top leaders.

Paul's prescription resorts to the fundamentals of the spiritual life, such as prayers of supplication and thanks, and perpetual rejoicing in the Lord. Minds occupied by these habitual disciplines find peace that passes understanding. The leaders would also not be able to rejoice and quarrel at the same time, just as "one cannot chew gum and whistle at the same time." Our sermon text, then, is Philippians 4:4, "Rejoice in the Lord alway; and again I say, Rejoice" (KJV).

A SERMON BRIEF
"Rejoice Always!"

My sister shared with me a quaint saying from her German neighbor: "Be sure to listen to people who sing while they work, 'cause *mean people don't know no songs.*" The saying seemed extreme at first, but the more I thought about it, the more sense it made.

Paul's admonition likewise seems extreme at first. Could he be serious about this business of rejoicing all the time? To find out, let's look at the context in which he says it. Two very faithful women of the Philippian church are not of the same mind. This is a gross understatement: their disagreement is tearing up the church. When it was just beginning, these sisters were dependable and hard workers. "But now that the church done growed bigger, they done fell out over somethin', an' they ain't even speakin' to one another." Paul is deeply concerned; Jesus just might be back any time, and here this leading church is all torn with dissension.

"Beloved, please do what you can to help these sisters settle this argument, so the church can get back to the work of the gospel. The rest of the saints are getting restless, and we can't cover up this struggle. The whole community knows about it. So we just have to find some kind of settlement to bring back peace and harmony. They both see themselves working for the Lord, but not together. And that makes it look like they are working for themselves."

Paul's most emphatic advice to his yokefellow (whoever this is), and to the church at large, is to rejoice. If you look at all you have to praise God for, you won't know how to hold your mouth to fuss at anybody. You can count your blessings or count your criticisms. But blessings give God the praise that is due, while negative statements make a sour face and drive people away.

Many years ago there was a member in our congregation who hated my husband with such a passion that she ordered him never to set foot on her property. We never found out why. But she did have one fine trait: she was an all-out worker for civil rights. One day my husband was running a big demonstration in one hundred-and-six-degree weather. This sister drove up beside him and gruffly ordered, "Get in this car before you kill your fool self." He obeyed and sat quietly watching her from the corner of his eye. What he saw was a woman too happy with the success of the demonstration to be mad at anybody. She tried to frown and failed. She had to break down and laugh as she drove him to the front of the line and wished him well. Rejoicing had taken the wind from her jaws and the meanness from her heart.

We fuss to let off the steam of our frustration and anger, and we use it to hurt and subdue people. We may say it is because we have to express righteous indignation, but our fussing is a weapon in a personal war. It is a way of putting people down, but it keeps *us* down.

In Dickens's *Christmas Carol,* old Scrooge discovers that the put-downs heaped on his bookkeeper only help destroy his own peace. When he is finally scared by ghosts into joining Tiny Tim in rejoicing, shouting "Merry Christmas," he is made happier than he has ever been. Perhaps the greatest really Christian aspect of Christmas in our culture is the fact that for many, it is the most joyous season of the year.

If we really want to bring peace and harmony, and help the family and the church, fussing will not do it, but rejoicing will. People do more good things because they are glad than because they are mad. Paul is urging the creation of a joyous Christian fellowship in which it is easy to do right, because one is already happy.

Then Paul follows the admonition to rejoice with a word about witness. "Be known to everyone for your consideration of others" (v. 5 REB). It is a powerful witness for the Lord, who will soon return. We can't afford to waste time and influence. Jesus' joy is contagious, and we are on "candid camera" all the time. If we do not witness for our joy in the Lord, we are witnessing for the reverse.

I suppose the most contagious joy and powerful witness I ever saw was at a university commencement. The governor had spoken, and the solemn assembly had moved to the reading of the names of the graduates. Suddenly a name was called, and a lady screamed, "Glory! Glory!" Her large white hat went sailing, and she shouted with an ecstasy such as few people ever enjoy. She herself would never have had such joy if she had felt compelled to hold it in. She did what Paul said and let it out.

One might have expected people to snicker and even laugh outright when that wide white hat went sailing. But nobody of the hundreds present cracked a smile. In fact, many shed a tear or two. One of these was the governor himself. It was plain that this was the first person in this lady's family ever to attend college, much less finish. It was plain that she had sacrificed much, and that her efforts had not been in vain. And some of us had to face the fact that we had never been that happy, partly because we had never felt free to express our joy. Joy isn't joy until you express it.

Paul's advice wasn't so strange after all. May you learn to rejoice in the Lord this Advent as you have never rejoiced before. And may your main joy come from the good news of God with us, starting at the manger.

SUGGESTIONS FOR WORSHIP

Call to Worship

LEADER: Sing, be glad and rejoice with all your heart!
ALL: **The Lord, the Creator of all life, is with us.**
LEADER: Be not afraid, O daughters of Zion.
ALL: **The Lord our God will give us peace and goodwill, for the Prince of Peace is come.**

Prayer of Confession

O God, like the children of Israel, we have strayed from the path of righteousness, and our hearts have enshrined the idol of material gain. We have treated Jesus' birthday as if it were our own, and we

23

have taught our children to seek for self, rather than to yearn to bring gifts to their Lord. We have rejoiced in small things given to us, and overlooked the true joy of our Savior, laid in a manger for our sakes. Forgive us, we pray, and teach us the true joy of Christmas, and indeed, the joy of praising you throughout the year. Amen.

Assurance of Pardon

We will give thanks to you, O Lord, for we thought you were angry with us, and now we know your anger has turned away (Isaiah 12:1). We will sing praises, for this day is come the Son of Righteousness, the messenger of your forgiveness. Amen.

Benediction

Joy to all, the Lord is come. Peace to all, the Prince of Peace is with us. Live now as children of grace, and may the love of Christ shine through you, this day and always. Amen.

Fourth Sunday of Advent

Sylvia C. Guinn-Ammons

Micah 5:2-5a: A prophecy that the Christ will be born in Bethlehem.

Luke 1:47-55: The Magnificat.

or Psalm 80:1-7: Israel's prayer for deliverance from calamities.

Hebrews 10:5-10: Christ sanctifies us through the offering of himself.

Luke 1:39-45 (46-55): Mary visits Elizabeth.

REFLECTIONS

Summer of 1981, I traveled with a group of seminary students and professors to the Presbyterian Seminary in Matanzas, Cuba. Here I was introduced to liberation theology and discovered how important the Magnificat is in Third World theology. It is read with a revolutionary cadence. Words from the mouth of a young girl are enough to turn the world upside down. Surprising words from a young maiden.

I began asking Mary questions. Why would you sing such a song when you should be talking about babies with your cousin? Where did you find such radical, political words? Do you understand the repercussions of these lyrics?

And so I began my sermon, a one-on-one conversation, women talking. One who has no idea what's ahead. The other living after Easter. This sermon took on a life of its own, promising something new and unknown, the way each pregnancy does.

A SERMON BRIEF

Mary, why are you singing? Child, you should be weeping. You're pregnant, betrothed to an honorable young man who knows this is not of his doing. Why aren't you sobbing on your knees, crying inconsolably?

Such a child yourself. Perhaps you sing because you are so young, but even children know when they have broken the law. You've seen how people treat those who break social mores: raised eyebrows, turned heads, chuckles whispered behind cupped hands. You will be shunned at best, stoned at worst. Have you noticed how the nice girls aren't quite so friendly anymore?

Poor one, have you any idea where all of this will lead you? Away from home for your confinement, next door to an inn of rowdy strangers, in a crude shelter for your first birthing.

Poor one, little do you know about that not so merry chase your boy child will lead you on as he goes about his father's business. Beginning at the temple in Jerusalem, it will end at Golgotha. Perhaps it is best you do not know the future. Sing on, little innocent.

But child, have you any idea what the words mean? How radical your lyrics? What makes you think a woman-child would be noticed by the mighty Yahweh, let alone magnified! Be careful who hears you. This could be blasphemy!

Naive and childish boasting is one thing, little maid, but singing revolutionary lyrics in Roman territory is quite another. Your song moves from flirting with sacrilege into a whole new arena of politically incorrect and inflammatory statements. You have entered a land where few maidens dare to tread, the land of politics and economics. You sing of God's strength scattering the proud. (Mary, the proud don't like to be scattered, haven't you heard?) You sing that God has put the mighty down from their thrones. (This might be good news to the powerless, but not to the mighty. How long do you think rulers will let you sing songs like this?) The hungry have been filled with good things, and the rich have been sent away empty. (The rich don't like to be empty, Mary. They won't sing along!)

Perhaps you should stop singing, child. Should this song capture the imagination of the poor ones, they will turn the world upside down. Mary, for your sake and the child's, keep a lower profile. Think a minute, is this the kind of mother you want to be—a troublemaker, setting this example? Will you rock your baby to sleep with lullabies like this and make him radical too? What if he remembers and teaches others, and it catches on, and on and on, so that two thousand years later the melody lingers and we must ask ourselves:

People of God's family, why are we singing today? What is there within the human heart that brings forth song when the news of this present world contradicts good tidings and cannot begin to define the meaning of great joy? And yet the song goes on. Why will it not be silenced?

Perhaps it is the power of expectation, having something to dream in the darkness. Birth is like that. And this is a song of birth, of a miracle incapable of rational description, a song staccatoed by the kick of tiny feet, a song filled with hope for a child yet unseen.

Young girl, how desperately we need your song! We need your song in hospital rooms and state rooms, in our kitchens and in outer space, reminding us of God's timeless refrain:

God is vital, active. . . . in today and tomorrow.

God is fresh as birth. . . . with potential as promising as a babe.

God loves justice, blesses the merciful, feeds the hungry.

God comes to us. . . . unreasonable, unpredictable, unbelievable.

God comes to us in the middle of tax season, to the poor ones, making promises yet to be fulfilled.

God comes to us in Jesus, and Jesus gives God a face.

This is the song. God is with us, then and now and yet to be. And because God is with us, there is something to look forward to, something unseen, something called hope!

There are children diseased and dying who paint rainbows and sing without reason. Or is the reason hope?

Old folks clean house and plant gardens between bombings in the war zones of our world. They have no reason to sing. Or could it be hope?

Hungry ones repair to their larders and find only two loaves of bread remain, yet they sell one and buy white hyacinths to feed their souls. They sing with half filled stomachs. Is this hope?

The world looks at dying and war and hunger, and cries, "There is no hope! There is no song!" But Mary sings pointing to rainbows and gardens and hyacinths. And the song of Mary echoes beyond disease and bombs and empty stomachs.

So, little Mary, sing! You're expecting. And we too shall sing of the unborn dreams kicking within us waiting to be born. "It isn't yet . . . it is yet to be."

For Mary sings of Jesus before his birth. But there is no question in her mind, he will be born. Mary sings of God's justice before righteousness reigns throughout the world, but there is no question it will come to be. In spite of the fact that the rich are still rich, the poor are still poor, and the hungry are still starving, justice is sung as a melody complete, already fulfilled.

God has already shown strength, scattered the proud, put down the mighty, exalted the lowly, filled the hungry. This has happened and yet . . . it hasn't happened yet. This is and yet . . . it is yet to be. Can it be the promises of prophecy grow as real and as hidden as the fetus gestating toward the fullness of time: Not yet, but yet to be? Not yet realized, but real? Not yet delivered, but pregnant?

We, the Advent People, are waiting, seeing the real world, but singing anyway. Singing with the blind, whose eyes are yet to be opened, because we know God believes in vision.

We, the Advent People, are waiting, hearing the real world, but singing anyway on behalf of the deaf, whose ears are yet to be unstopped, because we know God will be heard.

We, the Advent People, are waiting, dancing a stumbling sort of gait along winter sidewalks and honking our way down busy streets, because we know someday the lame will leap into the circle with our Lord, and the whole world will join the dance.

And somehow, in this sad and muted world, we are called to speak, no, we are called to sing on behalf of those who are dumbfounded. We are to sing because we believe God wills us to harmonize with the angels those old familiar tidings of great joy.

So sing, Mary. Go ahead, sing. Lead us in your song. Amen.

SUGGESTIONS FOR WORSHIP

Call to Worship

LEADER: O sing to the Lord a new song, for God does marvelous things!

PEOPLE: God hears us and remembers us with steadfast love and faithfulness.

LEADER: Make a joyful noise to the Lord, all the earth!

PEOPLE: Glory to God in the highest heaven, and on earth good news for all.

Prayer of Confession (in unison)

Holy child, born of a singing mother,
Forgive us our monotone lives,
for seeing darkness rather than light,
for hearing bad news rather than magnificent music,
for living with dread rather than delight.
Redeem us, enliven us.
Give us hope in our hearts and a song on our lips. Amen.

Assurance of Pardon

We need only ask and our prayer is heard. We need only hope and a promise is kept. God hears us and keeps us. Friends, believe the good news of the gospel. In Jesus Christ, we are forgiven.

Benediction

Christians, go into the world with a song in your heart. And may the God we know as Creator, Christ, and Comforter sing through you always. Amen.

Christmas Eve

Barbara Berry-Bailey

Isaiah 9:2-7: The prophecy of the reign of the righteous king who is to come. A reversal of fortune is promised to those who have been living "on the bottom," so to speak.

Psalm 96: A song of praise in hopeful expectation of the God who comes in judgment. In this psalm we do not fear the coming of the Lord, rather we sing for joy because God will judge the people righteously.

Titus 2:11-14: The declaration of God's mercy already having appeared in Christ Jesus. We continue to wait in hope of the coming of the Lord who has brought us back and bought us back.

Luke 2:1-14 (15-20): The (all too well known) birth narrative of Jesus.

REFLECTIONS

The hundreds of Christmas pageants notwithstanding, in our technologically advanced society it is truly difficult to try to recapture the mood of what really happened the night Jesus was born to Mary and Joseph. Imagine traveling all the way back to your hometown just to register for the census. (How many people fail to file their income tax returns on time, even with the advantage of filing electronically?) Even pregnant, weary, holiday travelers these days have comforts beyond Mary's wildest dreams. And as for that baby born in a stable, I am certain the birth got lost in the hustle and bustle of first century confusion. Even if word got around that someone had a baby, no way could that child have ever been the highly prophesied king, the one for whom people had been waiting. It was just the ill-timed birth of another child.

Yes, the birth of the messiah was a well-kept secret. And who is let in on it? Not the magistrates or potentates, but rather a couple of smelly shepherds even farther out in the boondocks who probably did not or could not register for the census (since they had no mailing address).

Who these days would believe or even want restoration to holiness to come to us like this? Who would believe "good news" that came to us in this manner? But that is how God acts.

A SERMON BRIEF

It's about ninety miles the way the crow flies from Nazareth to Bethlehem. It wouldn't be too rough a trek by automobile. But that is *not* how Mary had to travel. And Bethlehem was, after all, just some insignificant little town with not much going on. But the census made things happen; it made things come alive for a little while, and in the middle of all the commotion, somebody had a baby. Yet for the majority of the people that night in Bethlehem, it was just another night.

During my teenage years I grew quite disgusted with my father around the holidays. My parents were separated and I wanted to spend some time with him but could not, because he would always volunteer to work on all the holidays: Easter, Memorial Day, Fourth of July, Labor Day, Thanksgiving, Christmas Eve, and Christmas Day. He was a heating and cooling engineer at the Ford assembly plant just outside Detroit, and there was a tremendous amount of money to be made in triple-time pay—holiday, night differential, and overtime.

"How can you volunteer to work? It's Christmas!" I would argue every year.

"It's just another day," he would reply.

But Christmas Day was also my birthday, and for sixteen years it always got lost in the hustle, bustle, and shuffle of "the most wonderful time of the year." Maybe that is why I always want to connect with the Christmas story on a different level. There is something disconcerting about having your birthday come at a time when there is so much commotion going on. Somehow, the reason for your joy becomes insignificant.

Yet that reality also makes me want to pay more attention to the insignificant. Like looking for clues in a Sherlock Holmes yarn, I believe the answers are tucked away in what seems to be insignificant. And we gather here tonight because of a seemingly insignificant event that took place in an insignificant town.

Christmastime is an enchanting time of year, when stories of the miracles of Christmas are told by people who confess Jesus as Lord, as well as by people who have never set foot in a church in their entire lives. But even in the mystery of the birth of the Messiah there is a reality that gets lost: namely, that some two thousand years ago, two low-income, relatively insignificant people had something incredible happen to them. And because of that event the world is a different place. Not too many people were even aware of this birth and the ones who were, were pretty insignificant too. But since that time, people have died trying to pass on the story of this little baby named Jesus: who he was, how he lived, how he died and lived again, but more importantly *why* he was born, why he lived, and how and why he died.

I have said the word "insignificant" at least five times so far in this sermon. And I'll bet there are people sitting here right now feeling that way. Christmas is supposed to be a magical time, but for many people the festive nature of the season only exacerbates the misery they live with on a day to day basis, whether it be economic or psychological or domestic. I have been told that after victory in Japan and Germany, people in this country felt pretty important. But after Vietnam and a plethora of political scandals, after downsizing and drugs and teenagers dumping their newborn children in trash cans, it doesn't feel so big and bad to be an American. And what really drives home our insignificance is looking at photographs of the earth taken from space. I received one of these photos as a Christmas card. It was supposed to make me feel good, I suppose. You may have seen a T-shirt with that same photograph on it. It has an arrow pointing to a spot on earth and reads, "You are here." Such a view of earth is enough to make any of us feel insignificant.

But contrary to what that song said a few years back, God is not watching us from a distance, from where we would look insignificant. No, the God of whom we have heard tonight is about being here with us, close to us—yet in a most insignificant package—a baby. A baby born to a young teenage girl who had no social standing in the community, and who almost lost the man to whom she was engaged. But she was not insignificant. Though poor and of low estate, she was chosen by God. And she reminds us that no one is insignificant from the vantage point of God. Indeed, we cannot imagine the work that God can do through us, and the way God works to do it.

The Holy Spirit blew you here tonight. You may think you *only* came to hear the music, but something drew you to be in this place, at this time, with other people. You may not know them, but we all have a common thread running through us. Regardless of what we call ourselves, we have been called to this place to reflect on whether this Christmas is the same old, same old . . . just another day. Or is *this* the pivotal first day of the rest of our significant lives?

Mary and Joseph were real people with real problems. Yet they were faithful, and God cared for them, came close to them, and worked through them in a very significant way.

Don't let this Christmas be just another day. Be open to that same Spirit that blew you here, and let the Christ Child lead the way. Amen.

SUGGESTIONS FOR WORSHIP

Call to Worship
(by the Reverend Vivian Roberts)

LEADER: Sing unto the Lord a new song.
PEOPLE: **Sing God's praises in the assembly of the faithful. For the Lord enjoys our worship.**
LEADER: Sing unto the Lord a new song.
PEOPLE: **For Jesus is born this night in Bethlehem, and all of heaven and all of earth are rejoicing.**

Prayer of Confession
(by the Reverend Vivian Roberts)

LEADER: Almighty God, you caused our beginning. You have always been involved in our lives; you are always ready to receive us into your presence. You came among us in Jesus, our brother. Hear now our confession to you:

PEOPLE: **We confess that we are often more ready to respond to you in your house of prayer than we are to respond to you in our daily lives. Preoccupied with the successes and failures of our daily lives, we not only miss the opportunity to see you, but we also miss the opportunity to share your love**

33

with others. Forgive us, enable us to be more open to you, and guide us always. Amen.

Assurance of Pardon

Through the life, death, and resurrection of Christ, God cleanses us and gives us power to proclaim the mighty deeds of the One who called us out of darkness into light. As a called and ordained minister of the church of Christ, and by his authority, I declare to you the entire forgiveness of all your sins, in the name of the Father, and of the Son, and of the Holy Spirit. Amen.

Benediction

May the brilliant floodlight of the one who called us out of darkness shine on you, in you and through you, that you may go from this place and lighten someone else's darkness. Amen.

Christmas Day

LaVerne M. Gill

Isaiah 52:7-10: It is a time for great praise and rejoicing because Jerusalem has been redeemed. The whole earth shall see the salvation of God.

Psalm 98: A hymn of praise, joy, and celebration for the steadfast love and faithfulness of God. God is being praised as the one who will judge on behalf of the righteous.

Hebrews 1:1-4 (5-12): Jesus is proclaimed as the Son of God, superior to the angels and prophets. They are messengers of God; he is "the exact imprint of God's very being."

John 1:1-14: "The Word became flesh and lived among us." This is the theological foundation for John's Gospel, the coming of God in the human form of Jesus, the Son of God.

REFLECTIONS

It is always amazing to realize that the early church writers had to use so few tools to get across such a complex thought as the triune God. Not only did they have to be precise in their words, they also had to be persuasive and charismatic. No special effects, no computer generated images, no television talk shows to reexplain the inexplicable were available to them. Yet, they were able to carry the message to enough people and to convince enough people that today, even with all of the technology at our disposal, we continue to use as a basic text the words from those early writers.

The book of Hebrews is one of those phenomenal texts that shows us how very eloquent, yet methodical, the writer is in conveying the concept of Jesus, Son of God and messenger for a new age. Written more for the ear than the eye, it is believed that perhaps Hebrews was a sermon more than an epistle. The point to be made, and one that is made most economically with grand style, is that Jesus, the Son of God, takes primacy over the angels and the prophets who spoke in the past as from God. Jesus, the Son of God, speaks for God and is God.

Even as we greet this new millennium, the superfluity of words that have come over the last two thousand years pales into insignificance beside the economy of the Hebrews writer's prologue. "He is the reflection of God's glory and the exact imprint of God's very being, and he sustains all things by his powerful word" (Hebrews 1:3). Alleluia. Amen.

A SERMON BRIEF

My youngest son was born on Christmas Day at 2:48 P.M.—a time that brought unspeakable joy to my mathematician husband. The clock said 2:48 (two to the first power—2, two to the second power—4, and two to the third power—8). Needless to say, this put my husband in mathematical heaven.

This baby, like my first son, would change my life and the life of my husband. Neither of us took it lightly that he was born on Christmas Day, and just as we did with our other children, we had great visions of how he would change the world and how he would make a difference for justice in the universe. Though I would probably have fallen short of Mary's Magnificat, I could very well have stood in the street both times that I was pregnant and shouted great revolutionary predictions for change in the world order. Most mothers feel this way.

I say "most," because motherhood is not always a welcome event for women—especially not for poor, unwed mothers, engaged to be married, who find themselves pregnant by someone other than their intended spouse. In a place where choice is possible, such a woman might choose not to bear a child.

I often wonder what the world would say if today Jesus were to come to such a woman. Perhaps a woman like some of the women I have met in the homeless shelters or the dinner programs, or in the soup kitchens. What would happen if God chose them to bear a child? How differently would the world react? Would there be wise men coming from far away just to see this child, no doubt living in one of the ghettos of the inner city or in the barrios, or on the reservations, or in the Appalachian mountains, or in a trailer park? Is this generation ready for a Christ who would come under these circumstances?

It is on this Christmas Day that we should reflect on the story in which the "Word became flesh." It is the embodiment of the Word in the form of Jesus that we celebrate. And what has that Word been through the ages? The Word has been consistent. Whether it found its place in the Ma'at of the Egyptians, the Code of Hammurabi, or the Hebrew Bible, God has made known through many manifestations, that it is the oppressed, those that are held captive, the widow, the orphan, that deserve preferential treatment.

God's option for the poor and the oppressed comes through once again as this Christmas story emerges. This is not a story about gifts of material wealth. Indeed, it is just the opposite. It is about a gift of spiritual wealth, a gift so rich in spirit that it draws wise men and sages from near and far to witness the presence of the world's greatest paradox. A king born in a manger, a pregnant virgin, a son of God born of humans, a fully divine and a fully human baby. This paradox continues to confound the wise. So they come looking, but not knowing why God chose a manger and a poor Palestinian girl to bear the labor pains that would give birth to a child who would change the world.

If in this day and time God chose once again to bring forth Christ in the womb of the welfare mother, the prostitute, the crack addict, the homeless woman, the mentally disabled, the physically disabled, the poor, the destitute, ask yourself, this Christmas Day where would you go to find him? Do you know where these women are in your community? Do you know how to find them? If you knew, would you go and seek them out? If you knew that Jesus was their newborn baby, would you be afraid to go to the housing projects to see him, to the prison, to the barrios, to the ghettos, to the reservation? How much more different today is that trip than the one taken to the manger by the three wise men long ago?

Christmas is a time for joy, but at what expense are we joyous? As you open the gifts, as you repeat the story, remember that God chose Mary to bear Jesus.

SUGGESTIONS FOR WORSHIP

Call to Worship (Psalm 98 adapted)

LEADER: Make a joyful noise to the Lord all the earth; break forth into joyous song and sing praises.

PEOPLE: **Sing praises to the Lord with the lyre, with the lyre and the sound of melody.**

LEADER: With trumpets and the sound of the horn make a joyful noise before the King, the Lord.

PEOPLE: **Let the sea roar, and all that fills it; the world and those who live in it.**

LEADER: Let the floods clap their hands; let the hills sing together for joy.

ALL: **Let all the world sing praises to a just and powerful God.**

Prayer of Confession (in unison)

Gracious and just God, you cared enough to rescue us from our faithlessness. You cared enough to give us hope in the midst of our hopelessness. Yet we have failed to live as people whose spirits are renewed. We have failed to dispense justice wisely. We have lost our way, and we seek to be found and to be healed and to be made whole. We pray for personal wholeness and for worldly justice. In the name of Jesus Christ we pray. Amen.

Assurance of Pardon

LEADER: God has never left us. God has never forsaken us. God is with us. Believe the good news. You are forgiven.

PEOPLE: **Alleluia, Alleluia, Alleluia. Amen.**

Benediction

Go now, knowing that the Lord is with you. Know that the Lord is for you. Know that the Lord is here. Go now singing Immanuel. Immanuel. God is with us. Immanuel. Amen.

Epiphany

LaVerne M. Gill

Isaiah 60:1-6: The nations will come to Israel to see the shining light of the triumph and the glory of the Lord.

Psalm 72:1-7, 10-14: This psalm is a prayer for the king who is charged with meting out justice for the poor and the oppressed.

Ephesians 3:1-12: Paul ministers to the Gentiles because he has been commissioned by God through revelation.

Matthew 2:1-12: The wise men follow the star to find the "King of the Jews." After visiting with Jesus, the wise men leave by another road in order to avoid reporting to Herod.

REFLECTIONS

This time of Epiphany—manifestation—marks the appearance of Jesus to the Gentiles as represented by the wise men, or magi. These wise men are not enumerated in the text but are assumed to be three because of the gifts that are given. It is another wonder of the Christmas story that these sages would come from the East, noted for its wisdom, to witness the newborn babe's presence in the world. Not only did they come to witness, they also came to protect. When asked by Herod to return and give an account, the men changed their course and went home in another direction.

This appearance of Christ to those outside of the prophetic community is an affirmation to the world beyond the Jews that a new thing is about to happen. A new kind of king has been born: a king born of a peasant girl, a king born to give hope for a changing world, a king born to upset the status quo, a king born to turn the social order upside down, a king born to bring liberty to the captive and sight to the blind. In this manifestation of God a new thing is about to happen and it will confound the wise of the world.

A SERMON BRIEF

In Solomon's quest for wisdom (1 Kings 3:1-15), the Hebrew Bible says that he asked for a discerning *labab*. Translated, *labab* means mind or heart. This blurring between the words mind and heart has its genesis in the non-western Hebrew cultural context in which mind and heart are joined together as a repository of wisdom and compassion. Thus, Solomon's request is not only for wisdom in the traditional Hebrew sense; Solomon has asked for something else. He is responsible for the lives of many people, so many he can hardly number them. In this grand scheme of things, Solomon needs a new kind of wisdom.

What Solomon seeks, Jesus, according to Matthew's Gospel, already has. We find in the visit of the three wise men to the baby Jesus respect for their wisdom tradition, but also the recognition that they are moving from a point of prominence in the world of the wise to a point where they are only observers of the new wisdom. Jesus, the new creation in human compassion and wisdom, has been made manifest. He has appeared.

This epiphany is more than just the appearance of *a* Messiah, though. This is *the* Messiah, the one who comes as the Son of God to take away the sins of the world. He *is* wisdom and compassion. No longer will the meaning of wisdom be the same, and so the wise men pay homage to the future. They pay homage to the new way of knowing, the new way of revelation, the new way of performing signs, this time through miracles.

The wise men sojourn and make their way to the new keeper of wisdom, Jesus, by way of the stars. Avoiding all evil that may taint the journey and its purpose, the wise men refuse to take part in Herod's plot to kill Jesus. Satisfied with their encounter with the newborn babe, they journey home in another direction.

This new way of knowing finds its voice in the Epistles, as well. Paul, in Ephesians 3:1-12, tries to make it clear that his knowledge of Jesus Christ is not the same as that of the apostles. His knowledge does not come from books, from experience, or from being an eye-witness. His knowledge comes from revelation. It is the message from Christ through the Holy Spirit that creates in him a determination to be a prisoner for Christ Jesus, and that places him in ministry to spread the gospel to Jew and Gentile alike. It is a new kind of knowing. It is a new kind of being. Never again will knowledge, wisdom, and compassion be the same. Compassion will cease to be sentimental and placid, wisdom will cease to be contained in learning and studying, both will cease to be the province of a select few. It will be the possibility and availability of wisdom with compassion that will speak to the hearts and minds of many without a place in the society.

The wonder of the presence of Jesus, the ephiphany, the manifestation of Christ in the world as God's Son, is that hearts and minds will be touched by divine revelation through the Holy Spirit. The revelation of God's manifestation in the form of Jesus Christ forces us to recognize how grand this two thousand-year-old mystery is, even in this day and age.

With all our information technology, there is nothing that compares to the knowledge, the revelation, and the presence of the Christ-like mind and heart in the world today. It has endured for nearly two thousand years, and has yet to be replicated, contradicted, or proven to be less than true.

God made manifest to the world, the true wisdom. The true vine. Someone greater than Solomon has come. Praise God. Praise God. Praise God.

SUGGESTIONS FOR WORSHIP

Call to Worship (adapted from Psalm 47)

LEADER: Clap your hands and shout to God with loud songs of joy.

PEOPLE: For the Lord, the Most High, is awesome, a great king over all the earth.

LEADER: Shout to the Lord. And sound the trumpet.

ALL: Sing praises to God, sing praises, sing praises to our God, sing praises.

Prayer of Confession (in unison)

We confess now that we have not sung your praises loud enough, O God. We have not said "thank you" enough for the many blessings you have bestowed upon us. We have not witnessed enough to a world in need of knowing your goodness. We confess that our sin has been a sin of omission. We have left you out of our witness and out of our story. We ask for your forgiveness, God of mercy and of grace. Amen.

Assurance of Pardon

LEADER: Know that you are forgiven in Christ Jesus. That your sins have been removed by the birth and the death and resurrection of the only true Son of God, Jesus Christ, born of Mary. In this Christ, you are forgiven.

PEOPLE: **This is indeed good news. Amen.**

Benediction

We leave knowing that God, through grace, gave us Jesus for the atonement of our sins. We leave knowing that the light that was brought into the world with the birth of Jesus still shines for a world in darkness. We leave knowing that in Christ Jesus we have gained victory over death and been assured abundance in life. We leave committed to telling the story. Amen.

Baptism of the Lord

Susan Henry-Crowe

Isaiah 43:1-7: The language of intimacy and of distinction between God and people is the language of transcendence. "I am the Lord your God, the Holy One, your Savior." Because "I have redeemed you," there is no reason to be afraid.

Psalm 29: The psalm voices the grandeur and power of God. God is the One in whom the power to create exists.

Acts 8:14-17: The conferral of the Spirit comes in response to prayer. This text is an important companion to Luke's version of Jesus' baptism, in which prayer is central.

Luke 3:15-17, 21-22: Luke's focus in the baptism account, unlike that of the other Gospel writers, is not on John the Baptist or the Jordan River, but rather on the meaning of Jesus' baptism and its epiphany character. The voice from heaven is reminiscent of Psalm 29. The prayer life of Jesus is also significant for Luke and for the community of faith, in which being constant in prayer is crucial for receiving power.

REFLECTIONS

Luke's account of Jesus' baptism is different from that of the other Gospel writers. It is that which surrounds Jesus' baptism that interests Luke, not the ritual of the baptism itself. His focus is upon the community of the faithful, upon prayer, upon the appearance of the Holy Spirit, and upon a voice from heaven claiming the sonship of Jesus.

A SERMON BRIEF
"Surrounding Baptism"

For a moment, in a monumental experience, the focus is on the experience itself. Jesus is being baptized. But the writer of Luke astutely conveys that in Jesus' baptism, it is that which surrounds baptism that elaborates its meaning. In baptism—as in confirmation, in marriage, in death—it is all that surrounds the rite that fully gives it meaning.

I have a friend who, as a pedestrian, was hit by a car some years ago. The moment was terrifying, but all that surrounded the accident was what gave deep meaning to the event: the tender response of dozens of medical caregivers, the unrelenting anguish of his family and friends, the interminably long recovery with surgery after surgery to repair a shattered leg. It was the little things that were signs of hope and healing.

In like manner, it is that which surrounds the baptism of Jesus that helps us to appropriate a fuller understanding of baptism itself. Baptism is the first sacrament, the one on which all else rests. Jesus' baptism, although distinct from ours, points the way by which we come to understand more fully the gift of our baptism. In the Lukan account, emphasis is placed on three events that surround the baptismal moment: the beginning of Jesus's public ministry, the claim on Jesus as the Beloved, and a life of prayerful holiness that Jesus begins immediately following his own baptism.

Jesus' baptism marks the beginning of his public ministry—his public life and work. Through baptism Jesus is empowered for a life of service and mission. For those baptized in the faith there is no life that is not, in part, public life. There is no life that does not carry with it hope for relationship.

In his book *The Common Task,* Thomas Thangaraj addresses the meaning of this kind of relational living which derives from baptism.[1] Mission received in baptism has to do with "sending" and "going." It is both gift and responsibility. According to Thangaraj, "being-sent-ness" does not have to do so much with geographic movement, but rather is a quality of being. In other words, is it not so much where one is sent, but the attitude one carries wherever one goes. "Being-sent-ness" is dialogical and relational in character. And mission is that which happens in a network of relationships, thereby making the concept a relational one.

Thangaraj goes on to point out that mission is "being-with-ness."

Mission is carried out in the web of human relationships. It is a communal affair. It is response and responsibility. One cannot exist without the other. Mission cannot be authentic outside of relationship. By the same token, "going-forth-ness" is the response of the human to another. In "going-forth-ness" one discovers more fully the world, oneself, and God. "Being-sent-ness" and "going-forth-ness" are characteristic of those who have been baptized.

After Jesus' baptism, and from this point on, we see Jesus in relationship: to the Pharisees and Sadducees, to those whom he heals, to the disciples, to his friends. His public life is a life in relationship. It is the life of "being-with."

As an eighteen-year-old I learned about "being with" in the context of "being sent" and "going forth." Along with thirty other young adults, I was "sent" and went to Johns Island, South Carolina to work with migrant workers. These migrant farmers traveled from south to north most of the year working as stoop croppers, picking tomatoes and low-lying vegetables for eight to ten hours a day in the hot southern sun. My task was to care for their babies and young children in the nursery. But as with all works of love and mercy, the job description changes with the immediate or urgent demands.

Late one night a counselor came to get the two oldest women in my group to go with him. There was an emergency. We drove for miles out into the swamp looking for a lone shanty. Under the moonlit sky we finally came upon this small wooden shanty. Inside there seemed to be nothing, no thing save one rusty stove, one wobbly chair, a torn and dirty cotton-filled mattress on the filthy floor, and a sink. There in the dark, lying on the bare mattress all alone, in labor, just about to give birth to her second child, was a young Mexican woman of seventeen years. Knowingly and good-humoredly she instructed these novice eighteen-year-olds in what to do. Soon a tiny black head of hair began to emerge in the gush of uterine waters. There in the swamp, in a wooden shanty, on a moonlit night, in the midst of deep poverty of money, and in the rich spirit of life, there was born a child.

Hours, days, months, and years of reflection upon the experience and all that surrounded this birth provided rich and vivid meaning to "being-sent" and "going-forth." It was not my first nudge toward public ministry, but it was the most clear urge toward a life of "being-sent" and "going-forth." It was an experience, surrounding my own baptism, that urged me deep into the world.

The second sign of Jesus' baptism is the mark of mutuality and belonging, of being claimed and of claiming. The Holy Spirit says, "You are my Son, the Beloved, with you I am well pleased."

Affirmation surrounds Jesus and serves as a claim by God on Jesus as one who belongs to the realm of God. In these words we hear God's claim of acceptance, love, protection, and nurture. Jesus' desire for the Holy Spirit suggests a vulnerability and openness in his relationship with God. The claim requires a kind of response which yields mutuality. Mutuality carries with it an openness to movement.[2] It is because of his relationship with God, rooted in love, that Jesus is free to live in relationships and in the world.

One Sunday an infant was to be baptized and the minister invited the children to the baptismal font for the children's moment. He described what would happen and asked if anyone had any ideas about the nature of baptism. A five-year-old offered: "Well, it is like this. When the baby is in her Mommy's tummy she is surrounded by water that protects her, gives her the food she needs, lets her rest, not be bumped too much, and takes care of her until she comes out of the Mommy's tummy. When she is born, baptism is God's way of protecting her, feeding her, keeping her from being bumped too much, loving, and taking care of her." And so it is.

Lastly, prayer surrounds Jesus' baptism. In Jesus' baptism, prayer points the way to what a life in mission and mutuality requires. The Lukan account says, "when Jesus also had been baptized and was praying." Jesus' response to baptism is prayerful and involves holy living in community. Baptism is not simply a private moment or an individual possession, but the rite which signifies a commitment to a life of loving service in and to a larger community.

In the baptismal liturgy of my denomination, the congregation promises to "surround [the baptized] with a community of love and forgiveness, that [she] many grow in [her] service to others."[3] The church recognizes that prayer creates a sense of community and makes service possible. Just as prayer surrounded Jesus' baptism, prayer surrounds our baptism. Prayer makes the child's growth in the community possible. Prayer is the openess to being formed and transformed by the Spirit, by the community, and by the world. Prayerful and holy living replace prideful and arrogant living, forming communities that include genuine relationships of vulnerable mutuality and transforming love.

That which surrounded Jesus' baptism was transforming. In baptism, Jesus entered into life in a larger and more visible world. In the richness of being claimed for the realm of God, he would now enter into new relationships, rooted in mutuality and love.

Jesus exemplifies the kind of life that belongs to the Christian. In the rite of baptism, questions which are put by the minister to the parents of a child are equally appropriate for all baptized adults in the community. The pivotal question is "Will you live a life that becomes the gospel?" A life of loving service to the larger world? A life marked by vulnerable mutuality and transforming love? A life of prayer and holy living?

SUGGESTIONS FOR WORSHIP

Call to Worship

LEADER: Christ came to console the afflicted.
PEOPLE: **Come, let us worship our Creator and Comforter!**
LEADER: Christ came to empower the powerless.
PEOPLE: **Come, let us worship our Friend and Liberator!**
LEADER: Christ was annointed to bind up the wounded.
PEOPLE: **Come, let us worship our Redeemer and Healer!**

Prayer

O God of all creation,
You came into the world that we might know love and new life.
Pour your Spirit on your church,
That it may fulfill Christ's command to live the gospel everywhere;
That the proclamation of the good news might be heard throughout the earth.
Reassure us, that we are your beloved people.
Defend us against all evil and temptation.
Give us grace to bear faithful witness to you.
Endue us with love,
Keep us constant in prayer,
Empower us for the service of love.
Amen.

Benediction

Go now transformed by the work of love.
Go now in the assurance that the Spirit will uphold you for the work of love.

Go now empowered with the healing power of Christ.
Know that the world through Christ can be ours for the tending.
Amen.

1. Thomas M. Thangaraj, *The Common Task: A Theology of Mission* (Nashville: Abingdon, 1999).
2. Ibid. pp. 48-49.
3. *The United Methodist Hymnal* (Nashville: The United Methodist Publishing House, 1995), p. 40.

Transfiguration Sunday

Kathy Black

Exodus 34:29-35: When Moses returned from Mount Sinai with the tablets of the covenant, his face was shining. Moses then wears a veil when he is not talking to God or the people.

Psalm 99: God's holiness is proclaimed and God's presence in the pillar of cloud during the Exodus is remembered.

2 Corinthians 3:12–4:2: Paul recalls the veil image of today's Exodus text but implies that the veil of Moses (that is, the old covenant) is removed by Jesus so all may see the glory of the Lord.

Luke 9:28-36 (37-43): Moses and Elijah appear before Jesus while he is praying on a mountain. God's voice comes out of a cloud affirming that Jesus is God's chosen Son.

REFLECTIONS

The compilers of the lectionary paired the Exodus text with the text from 2 Corinthians because of the common veil imagery. But the reason for the use of the veil in the Exodus text is unclear. We assume the veil is worn either to protect Moses from the sheer radiance of God or to protect the people from God's reflected glory that shows on his face. But this is not so. Moses takes the veil off in the presence of God and when he is communicating with the people. He wears the veil during the ordinary comings and goings of his day. Paul twists this image around in the Corinthians text and uses the veil negatively, as a covering that hides shameful things. Finally, in Luke's Transfiguration text, no physical veil is mentioned. Rather, the cloud becomes a metaphor for a veil that neither protects nor hides, but represents the presence of God. These discrepancies make it difficult to reconcile the three texts.

The Exodus text is also paired with the Luke text because of the radiance/shining imagery. But in the Exodus text Moses' face was shining, whereas in Luke's version of the Transfiguration narrative, Jesus' face changes in appearance (the Greek word used implies that this happened in a natural way, as in our phrase "one's face lit up") but it is his clothes that shine unnaturally.[1]

Since it is Transfiguration Sunday, most preachers will probably focus on the Luke text. The words spoken by God from the cloud recall Jesus' baptism and the three disciples who have difficulty staying awake foreshadow the scene in the Garden of Gethsemene. Luke's is the only synoptic account that has Jesus praying on the mountain and the only one that speaks of his "departure" or as some translators put it, his "exodus" (v. 31).

We often stop our reading at verse 36, but verses 37-43 can also be included today. The story of the boy who probably suffered from some form of epilepsy should not be discarded, as we tarry on the mountain bathed in glory.

A SERMON BRIEF

"You are my Son, the Beloved; with you I am well pleased" (Luke 3:22). These words came at the beginning of our season of Epiphany when we celebrated the baptism of Jesus. Today we close the season of Epiphany with very similar words: "This is my Son, my Chosen; listen to him!" (v. 35). The Transfiguration text not only reaffirms what we learned at Jesus' baptism; it also sums up all the teaching and preaching that Jesus has been doing throughout this Epiphany season. God says to the disciples and to all of us: "Listen to him!"

But Luke's Transfiguration text is also a bridge between Epiphany and Lent because it foreshadows the passion and death of Jesus in Jerusalem. Verse 31 tells us that Moses and Elijah appeared in glory and were speaking about his departure—his "exodus"—which he was about to accomplish at Jerusalem. Luke wanted his community to know that Jesus' death was a great saving event, a spiritual liberation parallel to the physical liberation of the Exodus.

So what do we do with this text? We have almost nothing in our humble lives to compare to the glory and awe and wonder of this Transfiguration narrative. Jesus goes up to the mountain to pray and suddenly Moses and Elijah appear. Not only are they shining, but Jesus' face also changes appearance and his clothes become dazzling white. A cloud appears, and out of the cloud comes the voice of God.

Let's face it. There are very few in this world who experience the kind of Transfiguration that is depicted in this text—complete with dazzling rays of light, supernatural images of past heroes of the faith, and voices that resound from engulfing clouds. It seems so unworldly to us that while we yearn for that kind of a definitive religious experience, to put aside any doubts we might have, we also stand in fear of such unexplained glory.

But it is important to note that while Jesus' clothes did become dazzling white, the phrase used in Luke for "the appearance of his face changed" implies nothing supernatural. Jesus' face "lit up." And that is a reality with which we can identify. We know the feeling of seeing a child's face light up at the sight of a cake full of burning birthday candles, and we can remember the feel of the muscles in our own face when we "lit up" at the sight of one we deeply love. We use the term "radiant" to describe couples on their wedding day or a woman who is pregnant with a child for whom she has long prayed.

And like Jesus, we certainly have taken ourselves away to pray. Some of us have even gone to mountaintops. We have had various experiences of knowing God, experiences of peace, experiences of the holy. These encounters with the holy are often precious, rare moments in our lives. The trouble is, over time these experiences guide the direction of our lives less and less; they become dimmer and dimmer until they are almost hidden from our conscious view.

I live at the base of a ten thousand-foot mountain called Mt. Baldy. It looms large and majestic, surrounded by the foothills that guide our gaze gently upward until we fix our eyes on Baldy's often snow-capped peak—except, of course, for those days when it is so smoggy or foggy that we can't see the foothills, let alone the peak!

Sometimes God becomes hidden from our view because our lives are engulfed by the smog of the world and the fog of our own insecurities and doubts. There are wars and rumors of wars, tragic accidents, suicides, and terminal illnesses. There are job layoffs, marriage breakups, problems with children. And the radiance of that awesome God of glory and majesty can't be seen because there is too much smog and fog surrounding us.

Yet if we think we are the only ones whose engulfing fog creates doubts, the only ones whose faith wanes, the only ones who forget the glimpses of glory we have experienced in the past, think again! Peter was an eyewitness to this magnificent Transfiguration, but what does Peter do just before Jesus is crucified? He denies that he even knows Jesus—not once, not twice, but three times!

And the other disciples who had walked with Jesus and talked with him face to face, those disciples that sat at his feet to receive his teachings: what were they doing in the midst of this Transfiguration? They certainly weren't up with Peter, James, and John on the mountaintop. Rather, they were down in the village trying to do the work Jesus had called them to do. But they found themselves powerless to cure the boy who was convulsed by seizures. And when Jesus comes down from the mountaintop, note that he doesn't chastise the boy for his lack of faith; neither does he chastise the father for his lack of faith. Instead he scolds the disciples because, once again, they have failed to believe in who they are.

Jesus went away to pray, and during his experience on the mountaintop he came to know even more deeply not only who he was, but whose he was. This time of Transfiguration was not a conversion experience, neither was it the beginning of a new call for Jesus' life. After the Transfiguration, Jesus continued his ministry in attentive faithfulness to both God and the suffering humanity around him. He was not granted health and wealth and happiness, nor was trouble taken away from him. Instead, he continued his ministry of love and care and justice despite the pain and agony and even death that faced him in Jerusalem.

In a similar way, our encounters with the holy confirm our identity as disciples of Christ. But we too, get off track like Peter and the other disciples. We get sidetracked by the density of the smog in our lives and we lose our direction. The fog causes us to forget those experiences of the holy that claimed us as God's chosen, those moments where we know who we are and whose we are.

But what is fog except for low lying clouds? And in our text it is precisely in the clouds—in the fog—where the voice of God is heard.

SUGGESTIONS FOR WORSHIP

Call to Worship

LEADER: We come together today in awe and wonder before the God we worship.

PEOPLE: We also come burdened down with the worries of the world and the struggles of our individual lives.

LEADER: But in the midst of the worries and the struggles is God, our radiant source of love and hope.

PEOPLE: **We come together today in awe and wonder to worship the God who transforms our lives.**

Prayer of Confession (in unison)

Gracious God, too often we get so caught up with the demands of our families and obligations that we lose sight of you. We tend to make you fit into our time schedule and our understanding of how the world operates. We forget the times we felt closest to you; we lose sight of your glory. Infuse us with the light of your presence that we may be renewed once more. Amen.

Assurance of Pardon

The good news is that God never leaves us. We are not only forgiven, we are held in the palm of God's hand.

Benediction

Go now into this wounded world with the knowledge that God is present with you in the midst of the smog and the fog that surrounds your life, offering you hope and peace.

1. Jerome Murphy O'Connor, O.P., "What Really Happened at the Transfiguration," *Bible Review*, vol. 3, fall 1987, pp. 8-21.

Ash Wednesday

Janet Schlichting, O.P.

Joel 2:1-2, 12-17: The prophet calls the community to repentance and radical reorientation of its life toward God, who is gracious and merciful.

Psalm 51:1-17: A prayer for mercy: washing, cleansing, creation of a new heart and spirit.

2 Corinthians 5:20b–6:10: Paul, ambassador of Christ, urges the community to be reconciled to God in Christ's name. As in the book of Joel, the time is NOW.

Matthew 6:1-6, 16-21: From the Sermon on the Mount, Jesus' teaching on the practices of almsgiving, prayer, and fasting.

REFLECTIONS

For women in my Roman Catholic tradition, the "fasting" part of Lent presents particular concerns. Most of us under fifty never observed the old forty day fast of Lent, which was abrogated in the late 1960s and confined to Ash Wednesday and Good Friday. But the Catholic culture has always tended toward the idea of mortification during Lent, and so for most people, "What am I going to give up?" is still a prevailing question. There are still families that promise "No candy!" and we Catholic women catch ourselves thinking about beginning or resuming diets following the annual Christmas excess!

This can be a real trap, theologically, spiritually, and psychologically. What moves us to this practice? I asked a class of seventh graders in a Catholic school a question of this sort a while back, and the first answer was, "So we can suffer like Jesus did." Though Paul proclaimed the glory of sharing in the cross of Jesus, the early Christians knew this as a consequence of lived faith; they would have had no such answer in regard to Lenten practice. Lenten practices grew up, we think, in a several-centuries-long intertwining of the gradual moving backward of the two day Paschal fast, and the fasting and praying in solidarity with the catechumens during their intensive period of preparation for the sacraments of initiation.

My concern, particularly as an American woman tempted by the cultural tendency toward "the thinner the better," is that "thin is good" not be equated with "thin is God." This season may be the time for this tenacious weed to get its yearly pruning to the root. More important is the examination of our hearts and their hungers, and our world and its hungers, rather than our bodies, our poundage, our fats, and carbohydrates. Fasting must be relinked with its partners in the Scripture readings for Ash Wednesday; prayer and almsgiving, God and the neighbor.

A SERMON BRIEF

A friend of mine was shopping in a drugstore in early Lent, and stood behind a woman and a young child in the checkout line. There were the usual displays of batteries, chewing gum, and candy on each side, and the little boy was loudly insisting on a candy bar. "Not today," she told him. "It's Lent, and we give up candy for Lent." Then she turned to my friend and somewhat sheepishly said, "Actually, he's not mine, and he's not even Catholic. But I figure, if it's good for us, it's good for him."

Giving up. Is that what it's about? Depriving yourself? Six weeks of hitting yourself on the head with a hammer so that when you stop it feels wonderful? For a child growing up in the 1950s under the cloudy, winter skies of northeastern Ohio, Lent left an indelible impression: six long bleak weeks in February and March, long in-church devotions, and yes, no candy. It's still hard to shake; catch me off guard with the word "Lent" and I immediately conjure up grayness and grimness and gruel. Is that what it's about, really?

If we just concentrated on the single element of "fasting" in the readings today, we could get pretty stuck in the "if it doesn't hurt, there must be no merit in it" type of thinking. But if we seriously factor in Jesus' other two concerns in today's gospel, prayer and almsgiving, then we're forced to enlarge our concept of Lent, to move beyond mortification, understood as my own spiritual self-improvement and discipline. For that reason, I'd like us to consider Lent this year as the season of befriending.

Befriending: our soul, our body, our neighbor, our world, and by all of this, dwelling in God's befriending. By the practices of almsgiving and praying and fasting—which are not just for Lent but for a lifetime of Christianity—we do two kinds of befriending. We befriend the "Hole" and we befriend the "Whole."

First, we befriend the Hole. To be human is to have a hole—to be needy and somehow incomplete. As Augustine prayed, "You have made us, O God, for yourself. And our hearts are restless until they rest in thee." We have a difficult time living with this, "running on empty" so to speak, and coping with the fact that nothing will satisfy this vast emptiness but God. So we work very hard at filling it up with other things.

We dine on deli delights, tickle our ears with the latest CDs, and our nostrils with lemon-fresh, and dark-roast Colombian. We indulge our imaginations with computer games or murder mysteries, gorge our memories on sports trivia. We feast our eyes on big-screen TV. We crowd our closets with the latest fashions, our shelves with Beanie Babies, our desks with computer equipment. We fill our hearts with fawning friends and gratify our egos with praises. We cram our calendars with all sorts of important dates.

But it doesn't work. We're never full. We always want more. Lent is a time to face it. To go looking for the hole in ourselves, to reacquaint ourselves with it. To befriend it.

From the tales of the desert fathers and mothers there is a story about a young man who desired to join the brotherhood of desert monks. So he came to the desert and took up life in a cave, and soon sought out one of the wise old monks to guide him in this life of solitude and silence. The first thing he asked was, "Abba, teach me how to pray. I cannot. I sit and sit, I pore over the Scriptures, I recite the one hundred and fifty psalms, and say the prayers I learned as a child, but I do not think God is there. I do not feel God's presence. I find no peace. I wonder if God hears. What can I do?"

"Ah, well," said the old hermit, "here is what you are to do. Fill a basket with sand. And every day for the next two weeks, when you go to pray, pour a bucket of water over the sand in the basket." So the young seeker went back to his cave and did as the old man had told him. Two weeks later he returned. "Now, my son, what have you to tell me?" "Well, Abba, I have nothing but an empty basket. I went to pray, and poured the water on the sand every day, and it gradually all ran out of the basket."

"And that is what prayer is about, my son. Slowly, little by little, it is preparing in you a space. An empty space for God to enter."

There are various ways to enter into our own "holes." Praying, moving into our own silence, sitting with our own inability to "do," is one. And fasting can provide an entry too. For we can begin to see how much it bothers us to deprive ourselves. How much we think we need all manner of inessentials. How poorly we do, how grumpy we become, when we don't get what we want. What happens to me when I don't get praise? When I don't hear from a friend? When I pass up dessert? Miss my favorite TV show? When my car is in the garage or my computer is on the fritz?

In Lent we can meet not just our physical hunger, but a whole range of neediness which when befriended, makes for a wonderful God-welcoming emptiness. Wonderful? It is never, of course, a room furnished in high style, a space we'd imagine the Almighty would be impressed with, honored by. Strangely, the Almighty seems to prefer places that embarrass us, our vulnerabilities, and hidden shames. The holes and caves, basements and attics of a petty, puny race called "human"—this is where God seeks to settle, where God is at home. Lent is a time to make ourselves at home there, too.

Second, Lent is a time to look at our relationship with the Whole. The community. The Body of Christ. This goes back to Lent's origins, to the times when the Christian community began to fast and pray in solidarity with the catechumens as they approached their time for baptism. Fasting and praying were acts of unity, acts of hope, acts of pleading with God for new life for the elect and ongoing life for the community.

Almsgiving is another way of attending to the Whole. We do not live for ourselves alone. To care for the stranger, the widow, the orphan—these were commands of God for Jew and Christian to take seriously. By not doing so, they knew they betrayed who they were. Paul excoriated the Corinthians for "not recognizing the body," and so betraying their eucharistic identity, when food was not shared with the poor at their gatherings (1 Corinthians 11).

Alms are not just money. Alms are ways we share with others in need, reach out to help in whatever ways we can. Donations of food or clothing. A sharing of time or physical labor, like mending a broken window or carrying grocery bags. Offering a listening ear, or a cheering word, or sending a card. Alms are acts of love. Acts of connectedness. And they fly in the face of a culture of independence. God did not make us to go it alone. We are one Body. In God, we are a Whole.

Holes and Wholes. This Lent, befriend them. Give, or give up, as you wish. But the only point, and the only end of either, is Love.

SUGGESTIONS FOR WORSHIP

Call to Worship
(adapted from Joel 2:12-13; 2 Corinthians 6:2)

LEADER: Let us return to our God, with fasting, weeping and mourning:

PEOPLE: **And rend our hearts and not our garments.**

LEADER: For God is gracious and merciful:

PEOPLE: **Slow to anger and full of compassion.**

LEADER: Now is the acceptable time!

PEOPLE: **Now is the day of salvation!**

Prayer of Confession

Compassionate and merciful God, you call us to repentance and we gather here in your presence knowing it is dust we are and dust we have to offer. Take away our stony hearts and our leaden spirits, and give us new hearts and new spirits. Make of us a new creation, eager to love and serve you and our neighbor through Jesus Christ, our Savior.

Assurance of Pardon
(based on 2 Corinthians 5:21)

For our sake God made Christ, who knew no sin, to be sin, so that in Christ we might become the righteousness of God. Hear, and believe the good news!

Benediction

May God the Compassionate One bless us and keep us. May God's merciful countenance shine upon us and be gracious to us. May God look upon us with steadfast love and grant us peace.

First Sunday in Lent

Laura Loving

Deuteronomy 26:1-11: The offering of first fruits in the temple is the response to a history of deliverance. Storytelling buoys and impels the act of thanksgiving.

Psalm 91:1-2, 9-16: God is a refuge and fortress, and will command the angels concerning our safety.

Romans 10:8*b*-13: The generosity of Christ awaits those who confess Jesus as Lord and Savior.

Luke 4:1-13: Jesus, "full of the Holy Spirit," faces the challenges of temptation in the wilderness. Through his courage and steadfastness, we learn a way of being in the wilderness ourselves. The devil departs "until an opportune time." The passage ends with a cliff hanger, as if it were the season finale and not the opening day of Lent. Herein lies the drama of the Lenten season that unfolds before us.

REFLECTIONS

If there's any doubt that Lent is a dramatic season, let it be dispelled by the combination of texts for this first Sunday. These are great take-home stories, full of intrigue and suspense, full of confidence and groundedness in faith. The assurance one finds in the Psalm and the Epistle is genuine, and provides ample inspiration for preaching. The rescue from toils and snares spelled out in Psalm 91 is like a Greek chorus, reinforcing the wandering Aramean story of Deuteronomy.

The storytelling quality is what I have chosen to focus on in the Deuteronomy passage and the temptation account, because the nature of recounting the story is so different from what we do today. Today, if we were gathered around the kitchen table, we

59

would embellish the long journey through the wilderness, recounting in delicious detail the discomforts of the trip, the recalcitrance of our fellow pilgrims, and the general inconvenience: "Can you believe it? She wouldn't even eat the manna after all we had been through!"

And the temptation story? Don't even think about it! Whereas Jesus resisted the devil at every turn, I'm afraid we would have been bargaining, "I'll give you my whole set of Interpreter's Bibles if you'll stop quoting scripture," or wheedling, "I can't throw myself down from here, I just finished my nails," or using our problem solving skills, "Really, Satan, I sense that your demands come from a feeling of being squeezed out of a power position in the company. How about if we team you with Mary and Martha and see if we can't balance the power differential with the diversity of skills represented in your work group!"

We may sing the African American spiritual, "Lord, I Want to Be Like Jesus," but we may not have this temptation story in mind.

So what can we do to learn from the stories of faith that are presented here? We use them as a rehearsal, to practice throughout the days of Lent. For storytelling will be like a spiritual discipline for Lent.

A SERMON BRIEF

Every year on her birthday I tell our daughter the same story. "Did you know that I was in labor for thirty hours [the number of hours increases with each telling] before you were finally born by c-section?" I tell her about those hours on wrinkled sheets in a hospital bed inhospitable to a woman in labor. I tell her how we listened for the sound of the doctor's loafers in the hallway, how we read strips of paper telling us how "we" were doing. I say, "Megan, the azaleas congratulating you on your birth arrived before you did because the group sending them decided that surely you'd be here by now!" That group has been called "The Azalea Bunch" ever since.

And I tell her how we sang hymns as we counted out breaths and contractions—perhaps out of piety, or because we needed to conjure up ancestral voices to carry us on the tide of pain and possibility, or simply because those were the only songs to which we knew all the verses! I remember most vividly tapping out the ceremonious rhythm of "For All the Saints, Who from Their Labors Rest," grimacing at the pun on "labor" and remembering, in fact, the trials and tribulations of those who had gone before. When I wailed from the gurney en route to the c-section, "What did the pioneer women do?" a

Wagnerian chorus of blue scrub-suited hospital personnel intoned, "They died." "OK," I conceded. "Let's go."

That is the story of Megan's birth, surrounded by the communion of saints called forth as beacons from the ancient past and evoked from the sterile, white-lighted present, and called ahead from the shadowed future. For all the saints, who from their labors rest, I give thanks. For rest from that particular labor on March 19, 1982, I give thanks. And I offer the first fruits of this story of our firstborn as an offering on the first Sunday in Lent.

This is the way Lent should begin, with storytelling. Do you remember the one Easter vacation in Michigan when we went to church and the choir fairly resurrected themselves en masse from the balcony singing, "Up from the Grave He Arose"? Did I tell you about your grandfather's temptations in the business world and his ability to keep a code of ethics, a spirit of generosity, a sense of deep faith, throughout his lifelong career in business? Do you remember Ginny, battling for six years with the demon of breast cancer, and taking time to lift her weary head from her hospital bed and pray for her roommate, or her visitor, or her nurse?

What are the stories of faith from your childhood, your neighborhood, your family? Who were your heroes and spiritual mentors? How did the stories of the wandering Aramean and the other women and men who journeyed with him make their way into your repertoire of religious stories? Do they help you keep faith during your dark night of the soul? Do you gather courage from the stories of God's deliverance? Do you endeavor to get to the temple with offerings of thanksgiving when the journey is complete, in spite of, or because of, the vexing problems you had on the way? Or do you, as I do, lapse into the whining and self-referential tales of the journey, forgetting the grace notes, the glimpses of covenant fulfilled, the grandeur of a God who would pull a straggling band of refugees out of the desert and call them beloved.

And what of the beloved who wandered into the wilderness full of the Holy Spirit? What have you learned from the high drama on the ridge with Jesus and the devil? How does it inform the little dramas of ethical decisions in the workplace, power-jockeying in academia, the temptation to go for the easy way out in relationships, vocational decisions, and spiritual honesty with God? How have you arm wrestled with the devil? How has Christ been leading you "not into temptation"?

Let Lent be the season for recalling the stories of faith—the failures as well as the feats of courage. Tell stories of deliverance and thanksgiving, from ancient manna to your most recent rescue from disaster. If your father was not a faithful wandering Aramean but an unfaithful spouse with a wandering eye, then find the stories that do inspire, that do fortify, that do lead to freedom. If you cannot recount your own acts of courage on the parapet with the devil, then tell the stories of others, and learn from them. Tell these stories of faith, in your churches, to your children, through your actions. Tell them, as the Shema admonishes (Deuteronomy 6:4-9). Let this storytelling focus your Lenten journey. Let it fill your journal pages and your prayer life and the hymns that you sing. Pull out the text to Lesbia Scott's delightful English hymn, "I Sing a Song of the Saints of God" and remind yourself that the saints were "just folks like you and me." Write your own hymn texts, scribble poetry on the chalkboards of the church school rooms, offer to preach for a pastor who is burned out, arrange a storytelling circle with the elders in your church or community and listen to them. Let your lives and your congregation be so full of the Holy Spirit that these stories spring forth, bubbling through Lent, surfacing in newsletter articles and luncheon conversations and business decisions and bedtime stories.

Are you worried about preparing the youth for tomorrow? Coaching them for SATs, overseeing prom plans, making pre-birth preschool reservations, advocating for a HeadStart program in your area, mentoring a troubled teen?

Are we worried about honoring our elders, and the possibility that we might lose their voices and insights in the rush of daily life?

Are you worried for friends or relatives in mid-life transition, concerned that their compass has gone haywire or their center is off-center? Have you joined the baby boomers who are teetering on the turret in the wilderness and are prepared to throw themselves off just to prove that they have charge over the world?

Then tell the stories. They will bear you up like angels. They will not let your foot be moved. Like the promises of God in the Psalms, in the Epistle, and in the featured stories, they will bear you up.

Women, especially, need to tell the stories that have been lost or forgotten through time. When we tell our daughters (and our nieces and our confirmands and all the young ones who are not "ours"—nor are the ones we call our own) that the wandering Aramean was not the only one on the trip but there were women and girls along, too, then we hear the rest of the stories.

When we remind them and ourselves that historically the church took the bait and took on the temptation of power and chose to cast out those who were different, then the truth is told, the journey can continue, and we can still offer prayers of thanksgiving in the temple for the slow but certain deliverance of justice.

When we remind them that stories of deliverance went underground, and even now are crying out to be told, then the drama of Lent is heightened. There were stories woven by women into the tapestries that warmed the walls of castles, convents, monasteries, and mansions. There were stories laced in songs, from Hildegard of Bingen to spinning ditties, from hymns of faith to lullabies at bedside. There were stories stitched into abolitionist manifestos in early American quilts during the Civil War. There were stories that were buried in tiny quilts along the pioneer trail, and equally heartbreaking stories of broken promises and discarded treaties as indigenous women were displaced by westward expansion.

There were stories of triumph as women stepped to the altar and broke the bread of Eucharist for the first time, and stories of compassion as women ministered to the sick and the sorrowful.

Yes, we have lurched along in the wilderness with a mixed record on justice and passion and honoring the voices of the other. We have wrestled with angels and danced with the devil and we have won and we have lost. But we are still here, and God is with us, leading us with the torch of story through the wilderness. We are here, and God has called us to be midwives to the birth of the future, full of the Holy Spirit, cognizant of our past, breathing life, rhythmically, counting, chanting, singing, "For All the Saints, Who from Their Labors Rest." Thanks be to God. Amen.

SUGGESTIONS FOR WORSHIP

Call to Worship
(adapted from Deuteronomy 26:5*b*-9)

ONE VOICE:	A wandering Aramean was my ancestor.
ANOTHER VOICE:	He went down into Egypt and lived there as an alien, few in number, and there he became a great nation, mighty and populous.
ONE VOICE:	When the Egyptians treated us harshly and afflicted us by imposing hard labor on us, we cried to the Lord, the God of our ancestors;

ANOTHER VOICE: The Lord brought us out of Egypt with a mighty and outstretched arm, with a terrifying display of power, and with signs and wonders;

ONE VOICE: And God brought us into this place, and gave us this land, a land flowing with milk and honey.

LEADER: With these words our ancestors in faith brought forth the first fruits of the harvest.

PEOPLE: **With thanksgiving we, the women and men, girls and boys who dare to call ourselves the children of God, bring forth our songs and stories, our prayers and silence to listen for the Word of God, to offer praise and to celebrate the communion of saints.**

Prayer of Confession (in unison)

Loving God, we seek your face. Gather us up in your love as we confess our sin. We have forgotten the stories of the past, acting as if we invented trials, troubles, and temptations. We have failed to follow the model of Christ, whose life and ministry give us answers for the drama of our daily lives. We have resisted the whispers of the Holy Spirit urging us toward courage, praise, and wholeness.

So we seek your face, your embrace, your mercy. Turn us around. Make us whole with the freedom and forgiveness offered in Jesus Christ, in whose name we pray. Amen.

Assurance of Pardon

God seeks our faces, too, rushing to embrace the prodigal, rejoicing when the coin is found after the kitchen floor is swept, the last lost sheep is rescued, bearing us up on angel wings and offering us the gift of freedom and forgiveness. Receive the gift. Take it to heart. It is for you, and for your daughters and sons and grandchildren and neighbor children and all the generations of faith. Thanks be to God!

Benediction

Wherever you step, God goes with you.
Whatever the brink, Christ holds you.
Whenever the story is forgotten, the Spirit will remind you.
Go in peace.

Second Sunday in Lent

Barbara K. Lundblad

Genesis 15:1-12, 17-18: God makes a covenant with Abram, promising that his descendants will be numbered as the stars in heaven, sealed by the sign of fire pot and flaming torch.

Psalm 27: The psalm's image of shelter in the day of trouble, a place of hiding under the cover of God's tent, is connected to Jesus' invitation to gather under mothering wings.

Philippians 3:17–4:1: We hear Paul's strong promise that our earthly humiliation will be transformed and conformed to the Body of Christ.

Luke 13:31-35: Jesus weeps over Jerusalem for killing the prophets and stoning those sent by God. Still, Jesus longs to gather us as a mother hen gathers her brood under her wings.

REFLECTIONS

Jesus has been moving ever closer to Jerusalem since he "set his face" toward the city in Luke, chapter nine. We sense impending doom as some Pharisees warn Jesus to get away before Herod carries out his evil plans. But Jesus will not be stopped: he has "set his face to go to Jerusalem" (9:51) even though he knows what awaits him there. The heart of this passage for me is Jesus' poignant lament for Jerusalem. Before getting to the city, Jesus weeps over it for stoning the prophets who have been sent before. How Jesus yearns to gather God's children as a mother hen gathers her brood under her wings! But they have been unwilling.

We are indeed like the woman searching for one lost coin when we search the Scriptures for images that affirm women's stories and bodies. Jesus' image of the mother hen seems so small and homey, not big enough or powerful enough to provide safety from angry stones. I saw the mother hen trying to gather her children while the stones were flying and I began to think about stones: Joshua's stones of remembrance at the Jordan and John the Baptist's stones near the Jordan, stones from which God could raise up children of promise. Then I remembered the paintings in James Chapel during Lent: images of the mothering Christ gathering in the living and the dead in outstretched arms of mercy.[1] What happens when stones of remembrance and tradition are used to build walls or to kill prophets? Why is the image of "The Mothering Christ" so threatening? How does the image also bring life and gather in those who have felt outside God's promise?

A SERMON BRIEF

"Still I Long to Gather You"

(The preacher enters carrying a stone.)

When the children of Israel finally got to the Promised Land, they crossed through the midst of the Jordan River on dry ground. Joshua commanded the elders to gather twelve stones from the river bed; those stones were, no doubt, larger than this one. Stones to stand as memory: "When your children ask their parents in time to come, 'What do these stones mean?' then you shall let your children know, 'Israel crossed over the Jordan here on dry ground' " (Joshua 4:21-22).

The stones marked the place and held the memory of what God had done. These stones are important. They connect generations to the stories that would have been forgotten. They bear the wondrous weight of tradition when the whims of the moment make us forget that anything happened before we arrived.

I have no idea if Joshua's stones were still there when John the Baptist came to preach at the Jordan. But there must have been some stones by the river. Do you remember what he said? "I tell you, God is able from these stones to raise up children to Abraham." (We might add Sarah, too, though John forgot.) John was saying something about bloodline and tradition that day by the river. And he was saying something about stones: maybe the stones were not as solid as they seemed.

Now that was downright scary to those who trusted that stones were stones, to those who guarded the walls between insiders and outsiders. When fear sets in, we hold the stones tighter in our hands and shore up the walls of tradition. This is not only about Pharisees or Saduccees or others we would like to blame. It is not only about stones by the river. Stones are not always like this one in my hand. Some of the stones are words and rubrics: books of order, Augsburg and Westminster confessions, the Prayer Book of 1928, the constitution and bylaws of the Evangelical Lutheran Church in America. (Haven't you been told that some things are "written in stone"? That is, they cannot be changed.) These words handed down are important; I am not telling you to throw them out. They have outlasted generations. They have been passed down so that we, the children's children, will remember what we would have never known.

But stones can be misused. They can harm and destroy. The stones can become more important than God. By the time Jesus set his face to go to Jerusalem, the stone-keepers were anxious. For the one who was baptized by John in the Jordan had come up out of the water, God's own sign beside the river. Filled with the Spirit, Jesus was on his way—today, tomorrow, and the next day—casting out demons and performing cures, and raising up children of promise where outcasts had been. Before he even got close to the city, Jesus wept over it, wept for what had been and what was yet to come: "Jerusalem, Jerusalem, the city that kills the prophets and stones those who are sent to it! How often have I desired to gather your children together as a hen gathers her brood under her wings, and you were not willing!"

Oh, Jesus, what is a mother hen against the stones? We would have chosen a roaring lion, or, if not a lion, then an eagle lifting us above the fray. I asked a New Testament professor, since I did not want to say foolish things about the mother hen. "Sirach," he said. He sent me back to Sirach to listen to Wisdom's song: "She made among human beings an eternal foundation," but the Greek actually says: "She made *as a nest* among human beings an eternal foundation" (Sirach 1:15). Was Jesus holy Wisdom nesting among us? Can we thus say Jesus is Sophia enfleshed, or Sophia's child—even though the authorities in many churches have insisted that the name not be used in public worship ever since the reimagining conference five years ago?

Oh, Jesus, we have been warned: Don't push the mother hen too far. Don't make too much of her—as this painter has done! She has set your face upon a wash of aqua, of sea and sky, your arms spread wide to gather up all people, the living and the dead. But the face: is this face male or female? We can't be sure. The painter seems intent on leaving the question open. At the bottom, the title of the painting: "The Mothering Christ." But Mothering Christ is not written in the book. It is not in the historic creeds nor in our books of order. It cannot be found in the constitution or the bylaws. It is heresy! Blasphemy!

(The preacher faces the painting and lifts up a stone as if to strike it. Then there is silence.)

It is time to put down our stones.

O Jesus, still, you long to gather us. You come to us in ways that startle and surprise us. You are able, from these stones, to raise up names we had not dared to speak. Some of us pray night and day in words you taught us: "Father, Abba, Papa, holy is your name." These words are not only our strong rock, but close as our own breathing. Yet some have cried night and day for other words—not out of self-centeredness, but out of deep need and faithful yearning. "Mother, Sophia, Wisdom, holy is your name." And in the praying we were gathered under your wings in safety.

"Jerusalem, Jerusalem, the city that kills the prophets and stones those who are sent to it! How often have I desired to gather your children together as a hen gathers her brood under her wings." Oh, my children, won't you come? Don't be afraid: you can put your stones down now. Sister, won't you come? Brother, won't you come? Still, I long to gather you, says Jesus. Won't you come?

SUGGESTIONS FOR WORSHIP

Call to Worship

LEADER: Mothering God, you gave me birth

PEOPLE: In the bright morning of this world.

LEADER: Mothering Christ, you took my form,

PEOPLE: Your very body for my peace.

LEADER: Mothering Spirit, you hold me close,

PEOPLE: So that my faith can root and grow,

LEADER: Until I see you face to face,

PEOPLE: Until I know as I am known.

(Adapted from the hymn text, "Mothering God, You Gave Me Birth" by Jean Janzen, based on a text by Julian of Norwich. That hymn could follow the Call to Worship or the sermon.)

Prayer of Confession and Assurance of Pardon

LEADER: O God whose loving knows no ending, still you long to gather us under your wings. For the words of hatred we have spoken and the words of love we have withheld:

PEOPLE: **O God, forgive us and gather us under your wings of mercy.**

LEADER: For the walls we have built up and the barriers we have refused to take down,

PEOPLE: **O God, forgive us and gather us under your wings of mercy.**

LEADER: For the greed which makes us frantic and the gifts we pass by without seeing,

PEOPLE: **O God, forgive us and gather us under your wings of mercy.**

LEADER: For what we have done and for what we have left undone,

PEOPLE: **O God, forgive us and gather us under your wings of mercy.**

LEADER: Sisters and brothers, God's promise of mercy is sure: you are forgiven and loved as you are. Come now and rest under God's sheltering wings and know that you are home. (All sing together the refrain of the hymn, "Softly and Tenderly, Jesus Is Calling.")

Benediction

Like an eagle lifting up her weary children, God will carry you.
Like a mother hen gathering her brood, Jesus Christ will shelter you.
"Like the murmur of the dove's song," the Holy Spirit will dwell with you.[2]
Do not be afraid. Go forth in God's peace. Amen.

---

1. "The Mothering Christ" was part of an exhibit of paintings by Janis Pozzi-Johnson in James Chapel, Union Theological Seminary in New York, where this sermon was preached during Lent, 1998.

2. Carl P. Daw, "Like the Murmur of the Dove's Song," in The United Methodist Hymnal (Nashville: The United Methodist Publishing House, 1995) p. 544.

Third Sunday in Lent

Laura Loving

Isaiah 55:1-9: The promises of abundance, of covenant, of return, and renewal would lift the hearts of anyone. To a people weary from exile, these are words of life.

Psalm 63:1-8: The psalmist is eloquent in describing a thirst for God. This was written in the wilderness, and the liturgical rhythm that moves from seeking to satisfaction gives us a sense of an underground spring feeding the faith of the writer.

1 Corinthians 10:1-13: A review of salvation history is offered as a cautionary tale, reminding the congregation to stand fast when faced with the tests of their faith. Interestingly, the reflections on the ancient Israelites offer the images of strength gained from drinking the "same spiritual drink." Yet the ancestors were not exactly role models, and the spiritual rock from which they drank left them (in my estimation) curiously flawed.

Luke 13:1-9: This passage presents a harsh reminder to repent. The parable of the fig tree reinforces the imperative. Interestingly, this parable directly precedes the healing of the bent over woman, a text often called forth as one that reveals the rule-bending, liberating, hypocrite-seeking ministry of Jesus. Is the juxtaposition a Lukan balancing act? Will the real Jesus please stand up? Can we eat the fruit of the parable, drink from the living water, *and* find a way to stand up ourselves?

REFLECTIONS

I lived in Libya for a couple of years when I was growing up. The desert climate was tempered along the coast by the Mediterranean.

But further inland, the dry Sahara stretched on and on. The appearance of an oasis after a day in the desert was nothing short of a miracle. All of a sudden, out of the sand-beige horizon, the silhouette of palm trees, a knot of dark colors, and cool, beckoning shade. Coming closer one could hear the sounds of snorting camels and chattering children, clustered around the pond and the well.

The spiritual metaphor has the same contrast and intensity. There are days when one's faith journey is as desolate as the desert. There are times when God's renewing Spirit is as lifesaving as this cool, green reprieve.

This is the midpoint in our Lenten journey, an appropriate place for an oasis as we make our way through the wilderness. Our texts offer images of refreshment, spiritual drink, and a covenant that involves repentance. How do we reconcile those images that seem to pit the grace of underground springs against the requirement of transformation? I usually gravitate toward the thirst-quenching images, and believe that God's refreshment does not depend on my acknowledgment of thirst. But upon closer examination, the disparity between these two theologies may not be so great after all.

A SERMON BRIEF

The air was already hot on that May morning. My parting words as I deposited a vanload of teens at the gate of the amusement park were, "Be sure to drink plenty of water! You don't want to get dehydrated!"

I reflected ruefully on that remark as I drove away. Perhaps it's our North American hegemony that has us convinced that we should be drinking something at every available moment. Surely this is a cultural anomaly, a function of leisure and affluence and obsessive rehydration. Statistics of dehydration in other parts of the world teletyped across my brain. I was mindful of places where teens and toddlers face life-threatening shortages of water, where their lives are imperiled because of skirmishes over water rights, where dehydration takes its toll on livestock and lifestyles. And I disappeared into the air conditioned mall to escape the heat and get something cold to drink.

How deep is our thirst for God? Does it have anything to do with the proliferation of soda and juice machines on suburban street corners, standing like sentinels against the enemy, thirst? Would it account for the billions of dollars spent in advertising colored drinks in colorful cans? Could we explain to a person from another culture why we have cupholders on strollers and golfcarts, coolers in the cabs of combines, and flight attendants' who race to roll the beverage cart up and down the aisle of an airborne jet?

What is that "thirst thing" all about? The more we have available to us, the more we think we need. It surely cannot be about replenishing liquids in our depleted systems. Rather it is a systematic denial of the "real thing," the "real thirst," the vague, inchoate longing that the psalmist had ready language for and for which we have only vending machines.

The question from the prophet Isaiah challenges us across the centuries. "Why do you spend your money . . . for that which does not satisfy? . . . Seek the Lord. . . . call upon him" (vv. 2, 6). Perhaps when we reach for the cold drink, when we seek out the illuminated soda sentry at the gas station or the break room or the hallway at school we are on another search.

That is where we find ourselves in this midpoint in Lent, searching for something, yet not quite sure what it is. We like the idea of oasis, of constant underground springs, of refreshment in the desert, but are we willing to admit our very deep and considerable thirst?

That would be repentance. That would mean admitting to ourselves, and to others, our absolute need for God. It would mean admitting that we cannot get through our day at the amusement park, through our class schedule, through our work, our life, without the cooling springs of God. That would mean, God forbid, that we are dependent. Radically dependent on God to replenish our spiritual cells, to refresh our hearts, to wash away our fears, to soothe our fevered brow. That would be repentance.

And that would be an appropriate admission, confession, affirmation of faith, cry of rejoicing, and of our need here in the midst of the desert of Lent. Just admit it.

And all of a sudden, the silhouette of palm trees, a knot of dark colors, and cool, beckoning shade. The presence of God, refreshing and splashing and beckoning and still-pooling for reflection and centering and deepening as the bucket goes down into the well and camels are noisy and children are chattering and we are in the midst of the oasis of God. Why are we here? Why are we privileged by God's presence when others are thirsting, really thirsting? Are we here to gather strength for the political battles that result in water rights being settled, in wealth being distributed, in vaccines and clean water preventing total decimation through dehydration? Are we here to pray for the other? To repent of our cultural hegemony that assumes thirst is as easily assuaged as it is in our cola consuming culture? Or maybe today, you are here in the oasis, not to do anything, but to rest and receive. Maybe you have fought those political skirmishes for distributive justice. Maybe you are weary from believing that you can single-handedly bring in the oasis of God. Maybe you just need to rest and remember who you are, and whose you are.

Before I dropped the kids off at the amusement park, I insisted that they carry some form of identification. "Why?" they challenged. I reminded them that we were in a different state, that if anything happened to them (like passing out from dehydration) someone would know who they were. "It's important to know who you are and where you're from," I added. Right before I told them about drinking water.

Yes, we have too much. Yes, we continue to thirst in a vague and inarticulate way. But we are beginning to remember who we are and whose we are. I think it is an organic reaction, this self-knowledge, this sense of identity. It comes from our cells being filled with the springs of God, from drawing deep from the well and eagerly drinking the draughts of holy water.

Remember who you are. And drink plenty of water.

SUGGESTIONS FOR WORSHIP

Call to Worship (Psalm 63:1-4)

LEADER: God, you are my God, I seek you, my soul thirsts for you.

PEOPLE: **My flesh faints for you, as in a dry and weary land where there is no water.**

LEADER: So I have looked upon you in the sanctuary, beholding your power and glory.

PEOPLE: **Because your steadfast love is better than life, my lips will praise you.**

LEADER: So I will bless you as long as I live;

PEOPLE: **I will lift up my hands and call on your name.**

Prayer of Confession (in unison)

O God, in the words of worship we call on your name. But in the rest of our lives, we refuse to acknowledge our dependence on you.

We have struggled to be self-sufficient, independent, not to need anyone. Yet we need you, and we will not admit it.

So let the water of your grace seep into our hardened hearts. Let it run through our walls of resistance, spilling and splashing with possibility and peace at last. Refresh us, O God, even as you wash away our faults. We pray in the name of the Living Water, Jesus Christ. Amen.

Assurance of Pardon

You have made the journey to the oasis. Now receive its renewal.
The deep well of God offers you freedom from thirst.
Draw the bucket, take the water of life.
God has refreshed you with grace and mercy.
Thanks be to God!

Benediction

LEADER: Look, on the horizon. A silhouette of palm trees, a knot of dark colors, and cool, beckoning shade.

PEOPLE: **It is the oasis of God, calling us to come and be refreshed, calling us to be fully who we are.**

LEADER: Go from this place with your thirst quenched and your identity certain. God has claimed you and sent you forth as water in a thirsty world.

PEOPLE: **Thanks be to God, who satisfies our deepest longing.**

LEADER: Go in peace.

Fourth Sunday in Lent

Lynda Weaver-Williams

Joshua 5:9-12: These verses commemorate the celebration of the first Passover in the land of Canaan, which also marks the ending of the provision of manna for the Israelites. Thus, the gift of the celebration of Passover and its harvest connections replaces the gift of manna in the wilderness period.

Psalm 32: This psalm of thanksgiving, which has been used at times as a baptismal liturgy in Christian practice, expresses that through confession the penitent has found in God a "hiding place" of forgiveness and deliverance.

2 Corinthians 5:16-21: Paul's extraordinary words here reveal the heart of Christian experience: *katallagete*—be reconciled to God through Christ.

Luke 15:1-3, 11*b*-32: This richly woven text is one of Jesus' most well-recognized: the parable known as the prodigal son, or the compassionate father, or the resentful elder brother, or as Sharon Ringe describes it, the parable of the absent mother. There is story and sermon here, to be drawn from all the strands.

REFLECTIONS

I have read and heard a great many sermons about this parable. Most of them explore the human equivalent of landing in the spiritual lost and found. The theme of being lost and found is prominent in all three of the Lukan parables in chapter fifteen, and though the condition of being lost varies, the foundness in each case is accompanied by joy. Perhaps another approach to these parables is via the metaphor of the search and the joy that lies at its end.

A SERMON BRIEF

Muriel Rukeyser's poem "This Place in the Ways" begins with an invitation to a journey, yet like many such journeys it travels by way of the familiar. This "dark and marvelous way" is a path which intersects with the place "from where I began."[1] She echoes what poems and parables have told us for ages: to take up a quest in our lives is always, at least in part, to re-trace our steps, to explore what T.S. Eliot calls the "unknown, remembered gate."

A certain man had two sons; yes, and a certain woman has two as well. The story of each of those sons, of my sons, of any of our children whatever their paths, is one worth consideration. However, for each of the characters in Jesus' parable, as well as for those listeners so carefully described in verses 1-3 as "Pharisees and scribes" and "tax collectors and sinners" (we might do well to ask why this kind of detail is here while in preceding chapters more generic crowd descriptions were sufficient), there are similarities. Each is looking for something: the compassionate father is looking not just for the return of his wandering son, but also for the reconciliation of them all; the younger son is looking for "himself" (the text tells us "he came to himself"); the elder son searches for the securing of his place in the family and his father's favor; the Pharisees and scribes search for validation of their religious lives; the tax collectors and sinners are looking for . . . a place of welcome? a good party? the words of life? Who knows?

I pondered the intersection of searching, family, and faith late this past summer when I began to look for my birth mother. I had always known I was adopted, and had not been overly curious about those mystery parents of long ago and far away. But as important mid-life events loomed and my curiosity grew, I called the agency that had processed my adoption, Hope Cottage, in Dallas, Texas. Hope Cottage no longer receives infants into residential quarters; there is no surplus of babies these days. But fifty years ago they did, and I was one who spent almost six months awaiting the right match.

Within three months of beginning my search, my social worker came up with the name of a woman whom she was sure was the one. The social worker called her; my birth mother denied my existence. Tentatively, she relented and acknowledged that in fact she had given birth almost fifty years ago at the county welfare hospital to a premature infant girl who subsequently was assigned to a social service agency. Did she ever see me? Did she secretly name me? Did she wake up at night and grieve the choice she had made? And, most important to me now—the narcissistic question—does she *ever* think of me?

I named her, for reasons of my own, Mother Mary. I don't know why. It was getting close to Advent; I had always liked the Beatles' song "Let It Be," which says Mother Mary comes in times of trouble and speaks words of wisdom; it was better than continuing to refer to her as "birth mother."

Mother Mary has kept me a secret for all these years. No one living except her carries the secret that is me. There is no evidence that the birth father even knows of her private parcel. She carried me anonymously for almost nine months in her womb, and in a way, she carries me still, choosing to keep all knowledge of me within her. She has chosen not to see me or even to receive a discreet letter from me. In all probability, Mother Mary will die and take her secret about me to her grave.

Yet, my search has been fruitful. I did not find what I had hoped. But I did find something: I, too, like the younger son "came to myself." I realized what I needed to do in order to put my origins in order: I needed to bless this woman who gave me life and then gave me the chance to live it. Who knows why she chose one path instead of another? All I know is that blessing her brings me to know deeper the Source of my blessing.

I have always been drawn to that brief phrase in this parable which describes the younger son's awakening: "he came to himself" (v. 17). In Walker Percy's novel *The Moviegoer,* Binx Bolling, stockbroker, movie aficionado, psychic castaway in the world of New Orleans aristocracy, describes his own awakening: "This morning, for example, I felt as if I had come to myself on a strange island. And what does such a castaway do? Why, he pokes around the neighborhood and he doesn't miss a trick. To become aware of the possibility of the search is to be onto something. Not to be onto something is to be in despair."[2]

For all these characters, biblical and fictional, the search itself is crucial. It is the means by which awakening to the possibility of sacredness is embodied and realized. For me as well, the search for my origins was the means by which I came to terms, in a deeper sense, with the blessing and mystery of life.

During a break between classes, a student approached my desk one day. As she moved toward me, I judged her mercilessly. Her hands were soiled from what I later learned was printer's ink, evidence of the job that supported her efforts to study. Her clothes were stained, her hair messy, and she had not, I recalled, even passed the first exam. As usual, my judgments misled me. She nailed me with one question: can you tell me how to find the real God? We had been discussing the various descriptions and names for the divine in the Hebrew Bible and now she wanted to know how to find the *real* one, the reality behind the names, symbols, and anthropomorphisms. I had maybe two minutes. I told her, "If you seek after the real God, I believe you will be found." This was no time for scripture quotation, for theories of revelation, for theological holding forth. She needed a bottom line so I gave her one. I do believe her searching after God, her asking, seeking, and knocking, for surely that is what she did that day in class, is worthy. Maybe it is the one thing that is needful that Jesus speaks of in Luke 10:42.

The Lenten journey draws us toward "the dark and marvelous way" from where we began; it is a forty-day exercise in asking, seeking, knocking, and wrestling. It is a liturgical, spiritual, and psychic search. The steps that move Jesus toward Jerusalem also urge us forward to the well-known stories of scripture where we began, with which we struggle each Lent. Yet those stories and the search itself also hold the possibility of leading us deeper into the mystery. The Lenten path reminds us that we *are* onto something and that something *is* onto us.

SUGGESTIONS FOR WORSHIP

Call to Worship (based on Psalm 139)

LEADER: Where can we go from your spirit? If we ascend to heaven, you are there; if we take the wings of the morning and settle at the farthest limits of the sea, if we make our bed in Sheol, you are there.

PEOPLE: **O God, you have searched us and known us; you seek out our path; you meet us in the ways.**

LEADER: Even when we say "surely the darkness shall cover me," even there your hand holds us fast; even there you discern our thoughts.

PEOPLE: **We praise you for we are fearfully and wonderfully made; wonderful are all your works!**

Prayer of Confession

O Gracious God, who knows the deepest places of our hearts, forgive us when we forget we are fearfully and wonderfully made, when we pretend you are not at the end of all our searching, when we give ourselves over to the "whatever" of our culture. Remind us that your knowledge of us is wondrous not punitive, and that we are defenseless against your love. Continue to seek us out even as we seek your face.

Benediction (based on Romans 8:26-39)

May the God who searches our hearts, knows our minds, helps in our weakness, attends to our sighs too deep for words, and who is never separated from us, be our source and sustenance.

1. Muriel Rukeyser, "This Place in the Ways," *Muriel Rukeyser: A Muriel Rukeyser Reader,* ed. Jan Heller Levi (New York: W.W. Norton, 1994), p. 113.
2. Walker Percy, *The Moviegoer* (New York: Alfred A. Knopf, 1961), p. 18.

Fifth Sunday in Lent

Barbara K. Lundblad

Isaiah 43:16-21: The prophet brings God's promise of water in the wilderness to those who have known only exile, along with surprising news: "I am about to do a new thing."

Psalm 126: The psalm picks up the water image of Isaiah and ends with a benediction of certain hope: "Those who go out weeping . . . shall come home with shouts of joy."

Philippians 3:4*b*-14: Paul counts all his own best efforts as "rubbish" compared with the good news that Jesus Christ has "made me his own."

John 12:1-8: Mary of Bethany anoints Jesus' feet with costly ointment. Judas protests her extravagance, but Jesus commends her for preparing his body for burial.

REFLECTIONS

The mood is ominous as the story begins, for chapter eleven has ended with the religious leaders conspiring to find a way to arrest Jesus, and wondering if he would come to the festival. Now the countdown has begun: six days before the festival Jesus came to Bethany—very near Jerusalem. This anointing story, with variations, occurs in all four Gospels and it's almost impossible to get the others out of our ears. Only in John does the woman have a name: Mary. Like the accounts in Matthew and Mark, John's story speaks of anointing for burial. But unlike those stories, Mary anoints Jesus' feet rather than his head. This action recalls Luke's story of the woman who washed Jesus' feet with her tears, a story that says nothing about burial. John's story gathers up pieces of the others, putting them together in a new way. Mary can be seen as the first to model Jesus'

80

call to discipleship as he urges his followers to wash one another's feet in the next chapter. If there is any hint of a royal anointing here, Mary heralds a very different kind of king.

Amid many possibilities for a sermon I was most drawn to the fragrance of the perfume which filled the house. I thought of the staying power of certain scents, aromas which carry us back to another place and time. This sermon was preached at St. Michael's Lutheran Church in Philadelphia, a congregation deeply rooted in the community and involved in many justice ministries. I wanted them to be bathed in the fragrance of Jesus' presence, to remember resurrection's staying power in their daily lives.

A SERMON BRIEF

"The Fragrance Lingers in the Air"

Some say the sense of smell evokes the strongest memories, stronger even than sound or sight. I don't know if that is a matter of science or simply human opinion. But some things I do know. For many years whenever I caught a whiff of salty ocean air, I was back on the street where I lived in San Francisco one summer during college. In an instant I was pushing open the doors of the city bus and stepping out onto the street, then downhill toward my apartment on the corner. The smell of ocean air took me across the country from one ocean to another. The smell of ginger cookies baking takes me back to Grandma Lundblad's kitchen. She made the kind of ginger snaps that didn't snap at all. They bent—you could bend them almost in half without breaking. I cannot prove that the sense of smell evokes the strongest memories. But I know that certain smells are in my cells. What smells are in yours, beckoning places and faces and memories long forgotten?

I wonder how long the smell of sweet perfume lingered in the house at Bethany? How long did it last in Mary's hair? How long on Jesus' feet? Did Jesus remember the sweetness as he washed the disciples' feet a few days later? I wonder if Judas remembered as he led the soldiers to that certain place in the garden, money jingling in his pockets. (Was he planning to give *that* money to the poor?)

There is something strange about the perfume in this story: the fragrance which filled the whole house evoked memories *before* they happened. "Leave her alone," Jesus said when Judas complained about Mary's extravagant washing. "She bought this perfume so that

81

she might keep it for the day of my burial." But the story suggests that Mary had used up the whole pound of costly pure nard to anoint Jesus' feet. She didn't keep any for the day of burial; it was all gone, used up, wasted, according to Judas. Was Jesus saying that she had already prepared his body for burial? It was as certain as the smell of perfume which filled the whole house. It was in their cells.

Did Mary think of this anointing as a burial rite? Did she know that's what she was doing? If she wanted to honor Jesus or proclaim him king surely she would have anointed his *head*. Indeed, there are two other stories—one in Matthew, the other in Mark—where an unnamed woman did anoint Jesus' head. In those stories *all* the disciples complained about the waste of money, but Jesus commended the unnamed woman for preparing his body for burial.

There is also a third story, in Luke's Gospel, but it's not about burial. In Luke's story a woman crashes a dinner party. She anoints Jesus' feet not with oil but with her tears and dries his feet with her hair. What do we do with these differences? Was there one story told with variations or several stories with different women in different places? We have no way of knowing for certain, but this I know: the story of a woman who anointed Jesus filled the house! This story could not be forgotten. It filled the hearts and memories of early believers. It is remembered in some form by all four Gospel writers. John gathers up pieces of the other stories in his account: the town of Bethany and the anointing for burial as found in Matthew and Mark, the odd detail of a woman wiping Jesus' feet with her hair as found in Luke.

John's telling must be heard in its fullness and particularity. Yes, this anointing is for burial. But is it also a royal anointing? If so, Jesus is a very different kind of king anointed not on his head, but on his feet! In the very next chapter of John, Jesus takes off his robe, kneels down like a servant, and washes the disciples' feet. "So if I, your Lord and Teacher, have washed your feet," says Jesus, "you also ought to wash one another's feet" (John 13:14). A bit later Jesus says, "Just as I have loved you, you also should love one another" (John 13: 34). Was Mary the first to model this strange, loving discipleship? Did she understand that anointing Jesus as king meant anointing him for death? She doesn't say a word. All we know is what Jesus said—and that the fragrance filled the house.

Later, the fragrance must have filled the tomb where they lay Jesus' broken body. But when the stone was rolled away, the fragrance could not be contained. It filled the whole world as Lucille Clifton writes in her poem "spring song":

the green of Jesus
is breaking the ground
and the sweet
smell of delicious Jesus
is opening the house and
the dance of Jesus music
has hold of the air and
the world is turning
in the body of Jesus and
the future is possible[1]

We have come here this Sunday to break open this ancient story, to taste the bread, to drink from the cup, to touch each other with the promise of Christ's peace. Some will tell us it is pointless—extravagant—in the face of this world's needs. There will be days when we will do other things: we will do what we can to shelter the homeless, to open our doors to the children of this community, to defend the poor, and cry out for justice. God knows St. Michael's Church is opening its doors daily to bind up the brokenhearted and lift up the lowly. But today we will let the fragrance of Jesus fill this house. We will taste and touch and remember that Jesus has not gone away. Then, when we leave this place and go out into the streets, when we read of terrible tragedies which make us hold our children close, when we grow tired and this world threatens to wear us down, we'll hear the music of a hymn sung this morning, we'll remember the taste of bread and wine, we'll feel the embrace of peace, and hopefully, we'll be caught off guard by a whiff of sweetness in the air. What is that? Ah, then we'll remember the fragrance that filled the whole house— the extravagance of Mary and the extravagant love of God. The stone has been rolled away and the fragrance fills the whole earth. The world is turning in the body of Jesus, and the future, our future, is possible.

SUGGESTIONS FOR WORSHIP

Call to Worship
(based on Philippians 3:12-14)

LEADER: God, go with us on the journey,
PEOPLE: **God, stay with us through these days of Lent.**
LEADER: Not that we have already reached the goal,
PEOPLE: **Not that we have fully arrived,**

LEADER: But forgetting what lies behind,
PEOPLE: And straining forward to what lies ahead,
LEADER: We press on toward the goal of God's call in Christ Jesus,
PEOPLE: We shall never run this race alone. Thanks be to God!

Prayer of Confession and Assurance of Pardon (based on Isaiah 43)

LEADER: Let us confess our sin before God and in the presence of one another.
ALL: Merciful God, you have called us on a journey and promised to go with us, yet we have sought to go our way alone. When we try to go ahead of you, forgive us. When we lag so far behind that we get distracted, forgive us. When we lose heart, forgetting that you have promised to be near, forgive us. Come into our exile and bring us home. Amen.
LEADER: Sisters and brothers, hear God's word of promise: "Do not fear; for I have redeemed you; I have called you by name, you are mine." Your sins are forgiven. Your life is restored. Even now God's healing waters are springing up within you. Amen.

Benediction

Now may the balm of God's healing power anoint you,
May the fragrance of Christ's presence surround you,
May the wind of the Holy Spirit breathe within you and give you peace. Amen.

1. Lucille Clifton, "spring song" in *Good Woman: Poems and a Memoir 1969–1980* (Brockport, N.Y.: BOA Editions, 1987), p. 106.

Passion/Palm Sunday

Sylvia C. Guinn-Ammons

Liturgy of the Palms:

Luke 19:28-40: Jesus' triumphal entry.

Psalm 118:1-2, 19-29: The Lord's steadfast love and wisdom, and our doxology.

Liturgy of the Passion:

Isaiah 50:4-9a: The obedient response of the servant.

Psalm 31:9-16: Complaints to God for deliverance.

Philippians 2:5-11: Christ is our example for living the Christian life.

Luke 22:14–23:56: The Passover eaten and the Lord's Supper instituted.

or **Luke 23:1-49:** Jesus before Pilate; the crucifixion and burial of Jesus.

REFLECTIONS

Passion Sunday has always been a difficult one for preaching. As children, we want a parade. As adults, having worshiped through many Lenten seasons, we know where this parade leads, to Golgotha. As reluctant palm wavers, we might wonder about that crowd gathered to cheer Jesus into Jerusalem. What did they want from this man? Someone to rescue them? From what? Tired of waiting through generations of promise, and more generations of prophets, they erupt with impatience, "Hosanna! Save us now!"

We too want what we want when we want it! We expect it NOW! No journey through the dark days of transition, no entering into the pause of pain and passion between hosanna and alleluia, we want to jump from Palm Sunday to Easter. Like that first crowd, we fade into the routine of weekday living, unwilling to practice holy waiting, reluctant to engage in the depth of despair which blankets like fog the night before Easter dawn. Truly, we are of the lineage of this crowd.

A SERMON BRIEF

From a distance, climbing slowly toward the city, a small band of men push their way through palms and shouts from a noisy crowd. One rides a donkey. They make their way along a path downtrodden by centuries of caravans, downtrodden by conquering armies, conquered armies, slaves, and masters. A path downtrodden by sandals and hooves from around the known world, now kicking up dust with each step. Parched and sandy throats shout, "Hosanna, save us! Hosanna, save us now! Be you prophet, messiah, rebel, save us!"

The noisy ones spread their cloaks upon the path, wave leafy branches they cut in the fields, and begin shouting, "Blessed is the one who comes in the name of the Lord! Hosanna in the highest heaven! Save us now, now, NOW!"

If ever a generation were able to understand those people who lined the path of the first parade, it is we who are born into the NOW generation. It is we, the impatient people, who spend money we do not have, made easy by seemingly unlimited plastic credit. We want healing without the discipline of everyday personal involvement in our own recovery. We yearn to win a spiritual lottery and bank unlimited sums of instant faith, rather than save over a lifetime those precious moments which add up to a deep friendship with Jesus Christ. Yes, we understand the folks who stood along the route of that first parade shouting, "Save us now!"

I wonder what happened to that crowd? So enthusiastic, tossing their cloaks before a man and a colt, calling to their new hero. "Do it like David did! Make yourself king! Change things around here! We're here to cheer you on so you can save us. Hosanna!"

Jesus had the crowd in the palm of his hand. He might have used them to his advantage to gain political power, cause an uprising. His cause might have caught on, toppled the Roman Empire. He was the man of the hour, charismatic, calling the shots. But Jesus does a strange thing. Rather than rallying the troops to his cause and seizing the moment for himself, he rides on toward the cross. He rides on with a different understanding of time and a different definition of rescue. Jesus does not avoid the waiting and the weeping during his yearning time of faith. With novel insight into the mind of God, he is willing to wait with pain in the deadly darkness before the dawn.

Not so for the save-us-now people who wander off humming hosannas under their breath. They are off to find more promising messiahs to rescue them right away and give a quick fix meaning to their lives. Perhaps another leader, another cult, another car, another job, another drink, another baby, another cause, another marriage, another vacation . . . something that does not keep them waiting. Anything to avoid the weeping time, the yearning time, between hosanna and alleluia.

As the man on the colt rides off, the crowd does not follow. Most never know what happens a week later, never hear the alleluia dawn. Jesus rides on alone; through a noisy crowd, alone. Alone, he rides on to discover the meaning of this cup passed into his hands. Alone, he suffers. Alone, he dies. And because he learns how painful it is to be alone, he vows he will never, never leave us alone. "And remember, I am with you always, to the end of the age" (Matthew 28:20).

For seventeen brutal months as a hostage in Beirut, Lebanon, David Jacobsen knew what it was to be alone, yet not alone. Blindfolded, he spent most of his time on a cold dirt floor, chained to a wall. Eventually, he ended up with other hostages. They founded the Church of the Locked Door. Each hostage discovered togetherness in prayer, and each found that when the Holy Comforter is called, the Spirit answers. In confinement, the presence of God was stronger than ever, especially when they recited together Psalm 27, "Wait for the Lord; be strong, and let your heart take courage" (Psalm 27:14).

The hosanna crowd cannot wait. They wander off whistling "save us now" under their breath as Jesus rides on through the crowd vowing, "I will never, never leave you desolate; I will come to you and bring you peace which is not of this world."

No, the world cannot wait upon the peace of Christ. The world wanders away from the passionate week ahead, away from the waiting and the weeping and the yearning, looking for other messiahs to distract them from thoughts of death and loneliness and the long, difficult search for meaning.

Phillip Berman, author of *The Search for Meaning,* interviewed Americans from all walks of life, asking us what we believe in, what experiences have transformed our lives, and how faith informs our daily actions. He writes, "We arrive here, after all, with few clues as to where we came from and with even fewer clues as to where we are headed. . . . What matters, I believe, is the extent to which we have reflected upon our lives and acted upon the fruits of those reflections with sincerity, commitment, and courage."[1] He suggests our problem is that we are a practical people. We want answers, not problems, and when dealing with moral and spiritual matters, we discover mystery and find mystery deeply discomforting. Then we spend the rest of our lives avoiding confrontation with ourselves, distracting ourselves from deep reflection.

It would seem we have become masters of the trivial, tranquilizing ourselves with faceless values and shallow arguments. Perhaps we are victims of our own purchasing power, wealthy enough to buy those things which distract us from facing truth, a truth hidden beneath the superficiality of a cosmetic makeover, so easily acquired in our culture.

And so it is, the save-us-now people stand around somewhat bored, finally shuffling off to the rhythm of a halfhearted hosanna, kicking up dust and covering the prints of a donkey's path. Fair-weather watchers avoid the difficult search for meaning. Save-us-now folks have little patience with the ambiguities of life, so they turn their backs on the lonely man riding on toward the answer, and they buy into the mundane.

> And the people raise their voices, "Hosanna, save us now,"
> As he rides toward our salvation.
> "Can you wait with me he asks?"
> They wave palms and spread their cloaks upon the road.
>
> And the people raise their voices, "Hosanna, save us now,"
> As he breaks the bread and asks,
> "Can you share with me this cup?"
> They dance along the path drinking in the sunshine.
> And the people raise their voices, "Hosanna, save us now,"
> As he stumbles toward the place called "Skull."
> "Can you weep at the foot of my cross?"
> They shout, "Save yourself."
>
> And the people wander slowly off humming, "Save us now,"
> As he lay inside the tomb.
> Wait, can you hear the heavenly in the distant lifting dawn?
> But they could not; they could not bear the waiting prelude to the
> Easter Song.

SUGGESTIONS FOR WORSHIP

Call to Worship

LEADER: Hosanna! Blessed is the one who comes in the name of the Lord.

PEOPLE: **Blessed is the God who comes to us in human form.**

LEADER: Hosanna! Blessed is the one who comes in the name of the Lord.

PEOPLE: **Blessed is the Christ of God who comes to us, who lives with us, who dies for us. Praise to God for love so great!**

Prayer of Confession

Loving Christ, patient friend of the impatient, save us from our restless selves. Grant us holy moments within this passionate week ahead. Allow us time to ponder our souls, to ask forgiveness, to wait. Save us from the trivial which distracts us from the depth of your passion.

Forgive us. May the purple hues of Lent direct our gaze within. May all lesser gods fade as we prepare for the darkness before the dawn.

Assurance of Pardon

The Son of God, who drags his cross toward Golgotha, forgives all those who are truly sorry for their sins. Friends, we are forgiven people through the sacrifice of our savior, Jesus the Christ. This is the good news!

Benediction

Christians, go into the world to ponder the passion of our Lord. Be patient. Weep with those who weep. Wait. Be comforted, knowing that Jesus Christ, Son of the Living God, is with you always. Amen.

1. Phillip Berman, *The Search for Meaning* (New York: Ballantine Books, 1990), p. 5.

Holy Thursday

Janet Schlichting, O.P.

Exodus 12:1-4, (5-10), 11-14: God's instructions to Moses about Israel's observance of the Passover.

Psalm 116:1-2, 12-19: The psalmist praises God's saving goodness, wondering "What return shall I make?" The response links "the cup of salvation" with the Eucharist: "Our blessing cup is a communion with the blood of Christ"(1 Corinthians 10:16).

1 Corinthians 11:23-26: Paul recounts the story of the Eucharist and Jesus' instructions, "Do this in remembrance of me."

John 13:1-17, 31b-35: Jesus washes the disciples' feet, and commands them to do likewise for one another.

REFLECTIONS

We are not observers. This whole liturgy is for us and about us. It's about what we do, in yearly festival, in weekly worship, in daily life. Yearly, we tell again the great story of our redemption, the *Pascha* of our Lord Jesus Christ, and enact it in great solemnity. Weekly, we "do church": we gather around the table of word and sacrament to celebrate the Lord's presence in our midst. Daily we live that mysterious "becoming what we receive" in our being and doing for one another.

The story of the Passover, the story of the Eucharist, the story of the washing of the feet—yes, they are about the saving God and the beloved Son, but we are not detached hearers and spectators. The point is: it's *us* God loves and saves, it's *us* Jesus gets entangled with to the point of death on the cross. It's *us* the Creator, Redeemer, and Spirit pants for, pursues, rescues, washes, feeds, suffers and dies for, fills with new life, unites and inspires. And in the liturgy, stunned by such largesse, we ask, in the words of the psalmist "what return can I make?"

Of course, there is really no return possible. It's not about remuneration at all: it's about what happens when we, in Paul's words, "put on the Lord Jesus Christ." Our remembrance/*anamnesis* is far more charged than the words "making present" might convey. Consider yourself "plunged": immersed in the life of God, flooded with divine mercy, drenched in saving love, surfeited with the bread of life. We truly become what we receive. In Jesus, God has drawn us into the circle of divine life and love overflowing and that is now the life we live as church and as our truest selves: a life of "do as I have done, am doing, for you."

A SERMON BRIEF

At no other time in the church year does Eucharist reveal its meaning to us—and in and through us—so clearly and compellingly as on this day. This day, we gather in the upper room to celebrate with Jesus the Last Supper. And this day, Jesus shows us what it means to do Eucharist, in the intertwining of three actions:

The breaking of bread
The washing of feet
The dying on the cross.

Here this evening in the upper room, we are present as Jesus sums up his life, and we are given what we are to do as disciples; what we take on as we "put on the Lord Jesus":

The breaking of ourselves as bread
The washing of each others' feet
And the dying to ourselves that proclaims Jesus' death and invests the other actions with their ultimate meaning.

Each of the three actions tells us about the other two. We are food for one another, and we are water for each other's feet as we die to ourselves in Jesus. In all three, the stance of the heart is the same: "A condition of complete simplicity (costing not less than everything)."[1]

"A lifetime's death in love"[2]: This is what he gave us, and this is what we give back. A lifetime of washing feet, a lifetime of saying

91

"Amen" to the bread that is broken and a lifetime of becoming what we receive, a lifetime of putting on the Lord Jesus Christ.

The image I have is a garment, in which each of us has been clothed at baptism and which each of us is given to wear, even as we continue weaving it. Jesus provides the warp threads. Endlessly repeating, they are what he did, what he does for us always: break bread, wash feet, die on the cross. These are the core, the golden warp threads of our life in him. We provide the weft threads out of the dailiness of our lives—row upon row of varicolored, multitextured threads. All our lives we weave our Christian garment, in and out, over and under the washing and breaking and dying of Christ Jesus.

What do we weave? We weave being parents and children, being earners and learners, being loved and loving, cared for and caring. We weave our daily routines and the countless ways we love and serve each other. We weave in our daily wakings and bleary-eyed breakfasts when we patiently mop up the spilled orange juice; that act of kindness during the morning rush when we let the lane changer nose in; the countless tasks we perform with and for others: crafting, teaching, managing, selling, building, healing, speaking and listening, playing, preparing and gathering for meals. We run errands for the arthritic widow across the street. We volunteer at a soup kitchen. We listen patiently as Uncle George tells us that same old story. We bring the keys to a forgetful spouse who has locked them in the car. We offer to share that one remaining piece of chocolate cake. We make up after an argument.

We weave our communal moments: baptisms and birthdays, graduations and weddings, wakes and funerals. We weave our hard times: illnesses and sorrows, disputes and animosities, failures and losses. We weave moments of amazing grace: words of forgiveness, acts of uncommon kindness, glimpses of creation's beauty.

Daily, in human community, we weave our countless colors and textures. They are not always what we might hope. Sometimes the fibers are sisal-stiff instead of angora-soft. Sometimes there is undyed beige instead of royal blue. But we weave through Jesus' golden warp threads the fibers we bring, our own attempts at loving and serving as he did.

Having put on the Lord Jesus Christ, we weave with Jesus our garment. We wore it, small and new, at our baptism. We will wear it again, complete, in splendor, as our wedding garment at the great Feast of the Lamb, that is to come. For now, in these interim days, we wear it as we weave it, wrapped around our waist like an apron, like a towel.

And we, like Jesus, wash feet.

SUGGESTIONS FOR WORSHIP

Call to Worship (adapted from Psalm 116)

LEADER: How can we make a return for the goodness of God?
PEOPLE: **We break bread in remembrance of Jesus.**
LEADER: How can we make a return for the goodness of God?
PEOPLE: **We drink the cup in remembrance of Jesus.**
LEADER: How can we make a return for the goodness of God?
PEOPLE: **We wash each other's feet in remembrance of Jesus.**

Litany of Confession

LEADER: O God you hear our cries for freedom and rescue us from slavery:
PEOPLE: **Save us, O God!**
LEADER: O God you sent your Son as bread, broken for our deepest hungers:
PEOPLE: **Feed us, O God!**
LEADER: O God you gave your Son as love, poured out to quench our thirst:
PEOPLE: **Fill us, O God!**
LEADER: O God your Son knelt to wash our feet:
PEOPLE: **Cleanse us, O God!**
LEADER: God of mercy and giver of all good gifts, on this festival of remembrance, we praise you. You save us and feed us and fill us and cleanse us in Jesus, your beloved one, who laid down his life that we may live. May we live then, in joyful thanksgiving, proclaiming his death until he comes. Through Christ our Lord. Amen.

Benediction

Christ Jesus has loosed our bonds, he has filled our hunger, he has quenched our thirst, he has washed our feet, he has laid down his life. Go now, in the love of Jesus our Savior. As he has done, so may we do.

1. T.S. Eliot, "Little Gidding," in *Collected Poems 1909-1962* (New York: Harcourt, Brace & World, 1963), p. 209.
2. T.S. Eliot, "The Dry Salvages," in *Collected Poems 1909-1962* (New York: Harcourt, Brace & World, 1963), p. 198.

Good Friday

Melinda Contreras-Byrd

Isaiah 52:13–53:12: The words of the prophet foretell: that which is repugnant, despised, and rejected will become, to the astonishment of all, an honored source of empowerment.

Psalm 22: Reasons for praise somehow exist side by side with sorrow, suffering, and lament because of the delivering presence of God which surrounds human history.

Hebrews 4:14-16; 5:7-9: The human suffering of Jesus, our great high priest, connects all life, creating for us both a blessed legacy of redemption and a holy and loving vehicle for reconciliation and communication with God.

John 18:1–19:42: Jesus reveals himself as the Old Testament "I Am" and once again the truth of God repeats itself in history.

REFLECTIONS

The words of God's truth appear and reappear throughout history. It is as though they were created with special connectors that enable them to demonstrate the realities of God within the context of every circumstance and each generation. The people, experiences, and words of Scripture echo from Genesis to Revelation. Old Testament, which has passed, interprets New Testament which is to come; Jesus' birth, suffering, and reconciling life and death reinterpret the future of all humanity.

Timeless, reoccurring, ever-relevant, and universally applicable truths connect the varied readings for this Sunday. God is present in history. Things are not always as they seem or, more accurately, do not always end as they start. What seems weak may have real power. The unifying truth of these passages is that God's word is able to evidence its power in our life. God's paradoxical power is able to redeem the meaningless, and create new models for envisioning strength and power.

A SERMON BRIEF

"I am thirsty." Among so many important words stand these three seemingly unimportant words which come from the mouth of Christ as he prepares to die on the cross. Only three words among so many, they seem almost a passing thought. There he hangs, wooden spikes dug deeply into the soft flesh of his palms. He is drenched in perspiration and pain, a silent sufferer of the world's wrong. There he hangs, blood dripping from the holes in his hands and feet, flesh torn from the sheer weight of body pulling against the spikes. No wonder that having hung there for hours, body prey to the hot sun, he finally calls to those who stand looking up at him. He calls to those who gather around this horrible spectacle. He calls to those who might listen. He speaks those unforgettable words, "I am thirsty."

In such a situation thirst is to be expected. Why are his words unforgettable? Because he is not just another criminal dying for the wrongs he has committed. He is not just another man getting his just desserts. He is Jesus the Christ. He is the Messiah, the Son of God, who had declared himself to *be* "living water"!

He is Emmanuel, God with us, the Rose of Sharon, the Way, the Truth, and the Life, the final fulfillment of generations of prophecy. He is the Lamb of God who takes away the sins of the world.

Who is this man? He is Jesus, Savior, God Incarnate, and his words are the legacy of God in human flesh, dying for the salvation of creation. He utters these three words before his death and they are recorded and repeated throughout history. He is thirsty, and he is the Son of God. He is thirsty, yet he is the Son of God. He is thirsty, yet he *is* God!!

And this is the profound blessing of these three seemingly meaningless words. That he is thirsty means that he has completed the sacrifice of becoming fully human. That he is thirsty means that he has chosen to leave his powers aside and die the death of a human—for our sake, for your sake, for my sake. That he is thirsty means that he can feel, that he knows the full burden of being human.

His words then prove to us that we *do* have a high priest who is touched by the same fleshly weakness and temptations as we are. We *do* have an advocate who understands physical and emotional pain. We *do* have a Savior who knows what it is to suffer, and who struggled as we one day will struggle against the tyranny of death.

How amazing that although Jesus had the powers of heaven at his disposal he would choose to lay them all down and die in the powerlessness of humanity. He chose to come as the Son of Man, human as we are human, weak and limited as we are weak and limited. Yet he possessed the power of the universe. Human, yet divine. God, yet human.

And so Jesus knows the world we have created better than we know it ourselves. He knows a world where the Rambos and the 007s are considered heroes. He is not a stranger to a society that loves war movies and Star Wars. And he knows us too, the ones who inhabit this world. We are, after all, the ones who often anticipate the time when the cavalry will come riding in, shooting and burning everything in sight. We are the ones who want a God who will call down fire on the heads of our enemies. We are the Peters of the world who relish the chance to take up the sword and avenge a wrong. We are the ones who focus on Jesus' power to heal and to raise the dead, his kingship and authority, and forget he was also a nonviolent lover of children.

Yet he is the Christ, who models for us a new way of exercising authority and power, who embodies for us the cross-generational, repeating truth of God; that strength can be manifest in weakness. On the cross, he stood where we deserved to stand but could not. He had to be human to take our place, but because he was divine, our lives were saved.

We may prefer to sing about a Savior who could have called ten thousand angels, but we need to shout about a Savior who in tenderness and love could feel as we feel. We need to shout about a God who in all power, strength, and majesty would become flesh and dwell among us. We need to thank God for the fulfillment of this the ultimate holy plan: that the Creator of all things, our God who is the very essence of love, would see our pitiful state and come down through eternity so that though we are knocked down, we will never be knocked out. We need to be thankful that Elohim would come tearing the curtains of the temple, so that we who walk in darkness can see the great light! We need to thank God for the fulfillment of this, the ultimate holy plan: that Jesus Christ would come to die in a way that reminds us of the power of weakness; that Jesus Christ would come to die in a way that enables us to affirm that we have a friend in high places, who knows just how much we can bear.

I am so thankful for a thirsty God!

SUGGESTIONS FOR WORSHIP

Call to Worship

LEADER: He was despised and rejected by others, a man of sorrow and acquainted with grief.

PEOPLE:	**But it was his punishment that made us whole, his bruises that healed us. And we give thanks.**
LEADER:	He was oppressed and he was afflicted. Yet, he did not open his mouth.
PEOPLE:	**But it was through him that God's will was made to prosper. It was because of his anguish that we can see light—and we give thanks.**
LEADER:	He is our high priest, touched by our infirmities, suffering as we have suffered.
PEOPLE:	**He is our living example that God's ways are not our ways. He is the stone that the builders rejected that became the head corner stone. He is the last that became first. Through him we are challenged to live in a new way, to love in a new way, to lead in a new way—and for this we give thanks.**

Prayer of Confession

Ever-present, reconciling God, we confess that we do not with diligence listen for your voice, attend to your word, or search for your truth. We reject what is humble, ignore what is not loud, despise what is not lifted up. O thirsty God, reunite us with a Jesus-like kingdom-building humanity which will set our captives free.

Words of Assurance

The words of the once rejected now risen Jesus proclaim in jubilation, "O grave, where is thy victory? O death, where is thy sting?" Christ our great high priest has forever rearranged life's game plan. Because of Christ we are forgiven. Because of Christ we are free to live in newness of life.

Benediction

May the ever-present, reconciling, all-connecting God of history and grace be present in your life, giving new vision, holy continuity, and the ability to "count it all joy."

Easter Day

Karen Pidcock-Lester

Isaiah 65:17-25: To the prophet's question "Will you keep silent and punish us so severely?" (64:12*b*), God responds with a glorious vision of the new heaven and earth which God will create.

Psalm 118:1-2, 14-24: In this victory psalm, the community sings of the triumph which God has given them over the enemy, death.

Acts 10:34-43: Primed by a vision, Peter witnesses to the life, death, and resurrection of Jesus. Eager Gentiles, Cornelius and kindred, respond and the circle of believers widens into the world.

John 20:1-18: A drama in five scenes, John's resurrection account includes dazzling angels, tidy gravecloths, an erstwhile gardener, disciples racing in all directions, and a weeping Mary whose tears dry at the sound of her name on the lips of her Lord.

Or Luke 24:1-12: In Luke's account of the resurrection, Jesus does not make an appearance. But two men in dazzling apparel do, and they remind three women of what Jesus had told them. The women run to tell the apostles, who consider the report an idle tale.

REFLECTIONS

Whatever text the preacher chooses, whatever format the preacher uses, whatever audience the preacher addresses, the message of this day is clear: *in Jesus Christ, God has triumphed over the enemy, death, and new life in the reign of God has begun.* Through the words of the prophet Isaiah, the preacher can describe this triumphant life; through the psalmist's lyrics, the preacher can rejoice in it; through Peter's testimony in Acts, the preacher can proclaim it for all people, since now it is revealed that "God shows no partiality." The preacher can delight in the colorful details of John's resurrection drama and catch the light they throw on the story: What is all this running to and fro? How did the disciples go back to their homes after seeing discarded gravecloths in an empty tomb? How did Mary's weeping turn to wonder? Or the preacher can stand with Luke's three women at the mouth of the empty tomb and watch as the light dawns upon them.

The possibilities for proclamation are as numerous as the people who will sit in the pews on this Sunday. But with a story so familiar, even to those who grace the pews only once or twice a year, it is tempting for the preacher to try to find some fascinating detail that will dazzle with its newness. On Easter morning, as we celebrate the glorious resurrection of Jesus Christ from the dead, we must avoid the temptation of reducing this grand, vast mystery to some obscure fine point, however interesting it may be. We must proclaim that in Jesus Christ, God has emptied the tomb of its power: the resurrection is the central core of the gospel, and without it, "our faith is folly and we are a people to be pitied." This is a proclamation that bears repeating again and again, for it speaks to the timeless, relentless yearning of the human heart to be set free from bondage to sin and despair.

And once the proclamation that "Christ is risen!" has been made, the preacher may want to echo Jesus' own words after he declared himself to be the resurrection and the life (John 11:25-26), asking the congregation: "Do you believe this, or not?"

A SERMON BRIEF

(based on Luke 24:1-12)

"It seemed to them an idle tale."

It seemed to them the story of some grief-soaked women who could not see clearly or think straight. Ridiculous. Just talk. An idle tale.

It still seems that way to many.

What does it seem to you? Do you believe that Jesus Christ is not dead, but alive?

The question is not an idle one, not just something to muse and wonder about over coffee. You can muse and wonder over coffee about whom Cain and Abel married or about how all the species of animals fit into Noah's ark, and then clean up the coffee cups and go on with your day. We can live with those questions unfinished, undecided.

But not this question.

In this question, there is a great deal at stake. A great deal more than questions about death. What is at stake are questions about life and how we are to endure the living of it.

Because if this is an idle tale, then we must acknowledge that we live in a world where love—even the love of a man like Jesus—is sentimental and powerless. If the tale is idle and Jesus is not raised from the dead, then we live in a world where there is no power stronger than the sin that kills us—the greed, the jealousy, the hatred, the lust for violence that binds us like the strips of linen cloth bound Jesus for the grave. If this women's story is just an idle tale, then there is no power that can break those bonds, and we may as well be wound round with our own gravecloths, for the world we live in is "just a conglomeration of atoms with no grounding in moral purpose and history is just a scrambling for wealth and power."[1]

If this women's story is an idle tale, then we have nothing to say to a world in which children open fire on their playmates; we have nothing to say to the refugee stumbling across the border in Kosovo; we have nothing to say to the mother whose son has become a hissing stranger or the wife driven to a corner by her husband's blows or the friend who stands next to the casket of his dearly beloved wife. If this is just an idle tale, then there is no power that can lift us out of the abyss of hell, and our faith is futile, and we are a people to be pitied.

But don't try to tell that to the Christians in Hungary who were victims of the Hungarian Revolution in 1956, particularly the man imprisoned in a tiny cell, with hardly room to move, who etched in the plaster with his thumbnail a picture of Christ. Do not try to tell him that Christ is not alive and his faith is futile. He knows differently.

And do not try to tell Carmen, a refugee fleeing from her country, who lived in someone else's closet for two years and rode all day in a subway to keep from being a burden. When she at last got an apartment, she refused to accept any furniture besides the one lamp she moves from room to room. She says she doesn't mind the lack of light. She says she just wants her friend to sit down with her and read the Bible. She says the only light she needs is Jesus Christ. Do not try to tell Carmen that the women's story is an idle tale, and Jesus is not risen. She knows differently.[2]

For, like the women at the tomb, these people remembered what Jesus told them. And in remembering, the tale became not idle, but alive and true! The next time you find yourself entombed in darkness, remember what he told you. Hang on to it for dear life.

When the tale is no longer idle, but alive, we find ourselves living in a different world, a world that indeed may be filled with devils, but also is infused with a "deeper magic still."[3] And suddenly, since resurrection morning, we have something to say to those children on the deadly playground, or the mother who bears children for calamity, or the woman fettered by fear, or the man flailing in rage or grief or despair. And what we have to say is this:

There is a power stronger than whatever binds you to death.
That power is the love of Almighty God, and it was unleashed upon this life at the resurrection of Jesus Christ. It is *love* which is Lord of heaven and earth—not sin, nor greed, nor brutality, nor hatred, nor even death—and strong though these demons may be, their doom is sure. It is the love of God which will triumph in the end.

Friends, if the women's story seems to you an idle tale, if this day is for you a nice celebration of spring, something natural and lovely, when nature wakes up from its long winter sleep—then let bunnies and chicks speak for you at Easter.

But if you have found yourself entombed in darkness, and so you know that this story is not about the natural and lovely processes of creation, but about unnatural, supernatural powers that are terrible and fierce; if you know that the empty tomb is not about waking up from slumber, but about *standing* up against the powers of hell and *winning;* if you know that this story is not some idle tale but a declaration about *who it is that rules heaven and earth,* then don't settle for any silly eggs at Easter: grab hold,

and lift high,

a blooming,

empty,

cross.

[Liturgical suggestion: Rather than ending the sermon with the traditional "Let us pray," conclude with a strong call to "Let us stand and declare what we believe," so that the congregation actually concludes the sermon by doing what the sermon exhorts. One affirmation of faith might be Romans 8:35, 37-39, with the preacher calling the question in verse 35: "Who will separate us from the love of Christ? Will hardship, or distress, or persecution, or famine, or nakedness, or peril, or sword?" The congregation answers with the affirmation of verses 37-39, "No, in all these things we

are more than conquerors." Following the Affirmation of Faith, break into the hymn "Lift High the Cross."]

SUGGESTIONS FOR WORSHIP

[If possible, decorate the sanctuary with a "blooming" cross that is still shrouded in black as the congregation gathers for worship. To call the people to worship, stand in front of the cross.]

Call to Worship

LEADER: *[This part not printed in the bulletin, so that all eyes will be up front.]* Very early, on the first day of the week, the women went to the tomb. And they found the stone rolled away. And two messengers said unto them: "Jesus is not dead, but alive!" I proclaim to you: *[pulling off the shroud to unveil the blooming cross]* Christ is risen!

PEOPLE: **He is risen indeed!**

LEADER: Christ is risen!

PEOPLE: **He is risen indeed!**

LEADER: Christ is risen!

PEOPLE: **He is risen indeed!**

[Organist bursts into "Christ the Lord is Risen Today."]

Prayer of Confession

LEADER: Holy, Holy, Holy God, as we draw near to the mouth of the tomb and find the stone rolled away, as we bend with racing hearts to look inside, we are struck dumb. All our words are as prattle before the awe and majesty of your power. In silence, we bow before you, for we have fallen short of the glory for which you created us (silent confession).

PEOPLE: **Lord, have mercy upon us,
and make of us people worthy to be called your own.**

Assurance of Pardon

In the empty tomb, God declares that nothing can separate us from the love of God: nothing we have done, or left undone; no one whom we have been, or failed to be. *Nothing* can separate us from the love of God in Christ Jesus our Lord. Friends, believe the good news: in Jesus Christ, we are forgiven! Alleluia! Alleluia! Amen.

Benediction

Go into the world and lift high the cross,
for we have been to the tomb and found it empty!
Christ is risen, he is risen indeed,
and he shall reign forever and ever.
Let the people say: "Amen."

1. Richard Hutchison, "Reality and Resurrection," a sermon preached April 19, 1992, at First Presbyterian Church, Fort Wayne, Indiana.
2. The stories are drawn from the *1998 Mission Yearbook of the Presbyterian Church, U.S.A.*, and the format for telling them is inspired by an entry in that yearbook by Laura Mendenhall.
3. C.S. Lewis, *The Lion, the Witch, and the Wardrobe* (New York: Collier Books, 1986), p. 132.

Second Sunday of Easter

Barbara Berry-Bailey

Acts 5:27-32: Though given "strict orders" not to proclaim the gospel, Peter and the apostles fearlessly tell the chief priests they have no intention of obeying those orders, for they must obey God.

Psalm 150: An exhilarating song of unrestrained, unashamed, unconditional praise to God. Keep in mind the psalms were meant to be sung. Can you feel the kind of rhythm and melody a contemporary composer would ascribe to these words?

Revelation 1:4-8: A most reverent salutation to the persecuted churches in Asia Minor from John who is in exile. He, like Peter and the apostles, has been ordered not to proclaim the message of God in Jesus. This salutation is a bold confession of who Christ is (coequal and coeternal), how Christ is (so loving that he freed us from our sins by his blood), and what Christ is (Alpha and Omega).

John 20:19-31: The resurrected Jesus appears to his followers who deserted him at his crucifixion. They are huddled and "holed up" for fear of the Jews, but Thomas is not with them when Jesus appears.

REFLECTIONS

There is an old rhythm and blues song from the 1970s, "Have You Seen Her?" that comes to mind when I read accounts of Jesus' resurrection appearances. "Have you seen him?" That was the question of the week. Mary asked Peter; Peter asked John; all the disciples asked Thomas. We, as people of God, ask one another. In times of turmoil (hardly ever in times of celebration), we ask ourselves.

We consider ourselves followers, therefore we go to the places and the people and the situations we consider worthy of Jesus' presence. All too often we have walked right past where Jesus really is in our desire to put Jesus where we think he ought to be. I once heard a preacher say, "If you want to see the Lord, you have to let him be your Lord." He went on to say that in the overwhelming number of instances in the biblical accounts (with the exception of the apostle Paul), it was those who followed Christ incarnate who were the ones to see the risen Christ. It was true then and it's true now as well. Think about it. In whom have we experienced Christ? "Where were you? What were you doing when you saw Jesus?" That's how my mother would phrase the question.

A SERMON BRIEF

"Blessed are those who have not seen and yet have come to believe" (John 20:29*b*). When you stop to think about it, it isn't so difficult to believe without seeing. We do it every day. We depend upon the testimony of others to give us necessary and unnecessary information. Before television that was all you had: the testimony of someone else. Someone else saw it and wrote it down. You read it in a letter, a newspaper, or a telegram. As time went on you heard it through the airwaves, and now, thanks to telecommunications technology, you can see it as it happens.

And as we watch or read or listen, we know that someone credible and responsible compiled the story from credible and reliable sources and is telling us the truth, the whole truth, and nothing but the truth, right? Well, maybe at one time. But we have become a suspicious people, and rightly so. We are now discovering that, in terms of world history, not everything that was told was exactly as it happened, and what ought to have been told has been lost, omitted, or purposely kept silent.

In light of this reality in our own lives, we can understand and even relate to Thomas's demand for proof. Thomas wanted to see for himself. He wanted tangible evidence. Why? Well, because Thomas knew a great deal about the "credibility" of his cohorts. He knew about Judas, whose very display of love and affection was actually the sign to the soldiers to arrest Jesus. He knew about Peter, who insisted that he would *never* fall away, and then denied Jesus vehemently with curses and swearing when Jesus most needed his presence. Thomas knew his fellow disciples had not been very credible at all in the past. So maybe Thomas figured, "These guys will say anything."

After all, when Jesus first appeared to the disciples huddled and holed up in that house, Thomas missed out. And he refused to believe his buddies about what they had seen. He refused to believe his friends about what they had experienced.

Frankly, I think we owe a debt of gratitude to Thomas for his demand of proof. Without the physical test, those who heard of Jesus' postresurrection appearances may have wondered whether it was a ghost or the minds of the disciples playing tricks on them. Those of us today reading the story might wonder if Jesus didn't have the ability to produce a hologram. There was something strange about that body. But the touch on which Thomas insisted completely ruled out it being a ghost or a hologram. We don't get all the details of the how, but the testimony handed down to us by eyewitnesses gives us the who, the where, the when, and the why.

Jesus was standing there in the room, in the flesh, the same Jesus who was last seen crucified and gasping for breath on a cross. And Thomas saw Jesus. Jesus took the opportunity to speak those words that make possible belief and confession even apart from a physical visit: "Blessed are those who have not seen and yet have come to believe." And this account about the signs that Jesus did throughout his ministry and that day are written so that we, and others who hear this story, might believe that Jesus is the Christ, the anointed one sent from God to save us from the penalty of sin, and that through believing we might have life in Jesus' name.

The whole Gospel of John is written so that people may know who Jesus is. And we, who like Mary say that we have seen the Lord, or like Thomas who doubted, are called by the Holy Spirit and are gathered in assembly to hear the word, so that our faith might be strengthened through our physical encounter here with each other and with the risen Christ made present in the bread and wine.

And as he sent the disciples, Jesus sends us out to be witnesses to others who have not seen, heard, and tasted. Or to those who have, but who mistakenly think that once is sufficient for a lifetime, or that faith can be sufficiently nurtured on their own, apart from the community of disciples. It didn't happen with Thomas. The text shows us that this doubter came to faith in community.

In your own words, from your own perspective, tell the story of how God has moved in your life. Talk about how, when, and through whom the presence of Christ was made real to you. Talk about the day you saw Jesus. It does sound a little crazy at first, but think about what was going through your mind. Think about the joy or the peace or the comfort you felt. Think about how the fear that had paralyzed you, left you, and freed you up to face the challenges you conquered.

Remember the times you saw Jesus and go tell someone who needs to see Jesus too. What people do in terms of acceptance or rejection of the message is up to them. Our responsibility, our mission, is to tell the story—and to be faithful about telling it, remembering that just one time probably will not do it. We all need to hear the word more than once, especially in times of trouble or anxiety over those we love. Those who have built their foundations on shaky ground will definitely need to be persuaded more than once.

But in the end, it is the Holy Spirit that creates faith through the word. Give the word, and watch the Holy Spirit at work. For that work of the Spirit is something that cannot be denied.

It is somewhat ironic, the statement, "Blessed are those who have not seen and yet have come to believe." Because, when you reflect on it, *this* is most certainly true: Once you believe in Jesus Christ you really *do* see Jesus, and others see Jesus because of you.

SUGGESTIONS FOR WORSHIP

Call to Worship

LEADER: People of God, we have been blown together by the Spirit.

PEOPLE: Praise the Lord!

LEADER: The unfathomable God who created us and all that is has called us together in this place.

PEOPLE: Praise God in the sanctuary; praise God in the mighty firmament.

LEADER: Almighty God, the source of all our gifts, lives and reigns.

PEOPLE: Praise God with music and song.
            [Sing "Let's Just Praise the Lord" (William J. Gaither, 1972)]

Prayer of Assurance

Lord God, we give you thanks that you have created us and all that is. You sent Jesus to show us the way to eternal life. We pray that through your Holy Spirit, you would give us the courage to speak your word with all boldness, that those who do not see you at work in the world, nor Christ in their lives, may receive the gift of faith, may have hope, and may bear witness to the risen Christ. Amen.

Benediction

May God grant us, and all who hear the good news of God's love through Jesus, that sacred gift to see Jesus and to keep faith in the risen Christ. Amen.

Third Sunday of Easter

Karen Pidcock-Lester

Acts 9:1-6 (7-20): Saul, "still breathing threats and murder against the disciples," is struck blind on the road to Damascus and encounters the risen Lord.

Psalm 30: A grateful psalmist sings praise and thanks to the God who has answered his prayer, healed him, and turned his mourning into dancing.

Revelation 5:11-14: Every living creature in heaven and earth and sea declare, "To the Lamb be blessing and honor and glory and might forever and ever!" As John's apocalyptic vision unfolds, the text builds to a passionate climax with all creation looking towards the One who will open the seven seals.

John 21:1-19: In a "P.S." to the Gospel, the writer records a postresurrection appearance: despondent disciples go fishing, Jesus calls to them from the shore, they haul a fish load to the land, and have breakfast with him. Then Jesus talks with Peter, and instructs him to "feed my sheep."

REFLECTIONS

The ecstasy of Easter does not fade after the flowers have been removed from the sanctuary, for Christ is alive, and "he shall reign forever and ever!" And as these texts testify, he appears to his people in stunning deeds of power, drawing us up from the pit, girding us with gladness. God's mercy lasts a lifetime, and so it is meet and right that from the lips of God's people hymns of praise and honor, glory and blessing, still ring through the rafters and into the heavens and out into the world—even two Sundays after the Easter celebration.

In these lectionary texts, the preacher has a veritable treasure chest

109

of gems to hold in the light and reflect the brilliant message of the Easter season. Buried in the psalm, we find "Weeping may linger for the night, but joy comes with the morning"; "You have turned my mourning into dancing"; "O Lord my God, I cried to you for help, and you have healed me"—all of which capture in a nugget the glory of the gospel.

That glory is multiplied a hundredfold in the Revelation text, as all creatures of land and sea, together with elders and a myriad of angels, behold the glory and majesty of the Lamb who was slain, and fall down in breathless praise. What better response to what God has done and will do in Jesus Christ can God's people make in this Easter season?

However, if two weeks after Easter Day the preacher and congregation find themselves no longer breathless with praise, but rather, gasping for air in a world that knocks the wind out of us, then let them turn to the texts in Acts and John. Both give us accounts of what God is up to when life swirls on after the Easter revelry has packed up and gone home. In John, the disciples try to pick up their lives where they had left them when they had met Jesus: they go back to fishing. But it is in their ordinary lives that Jesus comes again to meet them, and ordinary living is no longer possible. In the story in Acts, persecution has replaced celebration for the disciples, and those who rejoiced at resurrection find themselves being murdered. Where is God in all of this? The story in Acts shows the risen Christ at work long after Easter Day.

A SERMON BRIEF

(based on John 21:1-19)

You may have heard it said that the theologian Karl Barth claimed that we Christians should read with the Bible in one hand, and the newspaper in the other.

This can be a grim exercise. We have watched in horror as Serbs order Kosovars to dig mass graves for their own people. We have shuddered in fear as news of high school massacres explodes upon us. What do we Christians, who read these newspapers with the Bible in our other hand, do in the face of such injustice, and poisonous, seething hatred? Turn the page and find the baseball scores and the supermarket ads?

What do we Christians do in the face of evil?

In today's Gospel text, Peter has stared into the face of injustice and has seen what hatred did to Jesus. What does *he* do when evil seems to have triumphed? Peter goes fishing.

What else was there *to* do in the face of it all? He had tried to make a difference, but he had failed. What else was there to do? So, one evening, sitting around with some of the other disciples, Peter, who never could sit still for very long, stood up and said: "I am going fishing."

The fisherman goes back to business as usual.

What else are *we* to do in the face of evil, when we too seem incapable of making a difference, because the hatred is alive and larger than life, because our own actions often betray our ideals and we are weak creatures who cannot keep *our* promises? What else *are* we to do when we look upon the face of evil, other than click off the television or fold up the newspaper, and go back to the business of living, as usual?

But Jesus stands in our way.

Jesus has a different answer. In our Gospel text, Jesus stands on the shore, interrupts business as usual, and calls to Peter: "Peter," he says, "there *is* something you can do. Feed my sheep."

No more can business be as usual. We cannot simply go back to the way things were before the resurrection of Jesus Christ. Christ is ALIVE! And he stands on the shore while we are adrift in our sea, and calls us to a life that is different than it was before we knew him. In the face of injustice and failure and hatred, the risen Christ breaks into our business as usual lives, and we cannot go back to our factories and labs and kitchens and classrooms and churches living as though evil has the final word.

Christ has risen! He calls to us daily in our ordinary lives, saying, "Follow me." Or, to borrow the words of the poet Wendell Berry, "Practice resurrection." In the face of evil, Jesus calls us to break from the world's ways and the world's wisdom that limit our lives, and let the *resurrection* define our lives.

I once had the privilege of chaperoning a middle school field trip to New York City. After a day filled with art and natural history, we climbed back into the bus at 5:30 P.M. and began to make our way through Friday rush hour. We squeezed our way into the clogged traffic making its way to the Lincoln Tunnel, and came to a standstill in front of the Port Authority building. There, in neon lights, were clubs with alluring names such as "Playland," where nude "girls" could be seen on stage twenty-four hours a day, where there were special men's

111

sections, where adult videos and reading material could be purchased.

I'd seen these places before, of course, in different cities. Such exploitation is as old as human civilization. But I had never seen them in the way that I was seeing them as we sat at a complete stop in the street before them. I never had looked upon the people who open the door and go in. I never had seen their faces as they come out. And I thought about the women—not *girls*—who were trapped inside. In a block such as this, surely injustice has a face, violence has a name, and evil speaks loudly and clearly.

But even in places such as this, it will not have the final word. Even for places such as this, Christ has risen.

And so it is that on the second floor of the corner building on the block, there are two signs. One, in tattered marqee letters, spells out "Jesus is. . . ." What Jesus is was hidden from my view, but that part is true: Jesus *is*. There is another sign which says "Upper Room Outreach Center: meals, shelter, clothing, counseling. Do come in."

In the face of the evil of this place, some fool Christians are practicing resurrection.

After Easter, Jesus comes to us and calls us to practice resurrection, with no expectation of being perfect. Peter's days of poor judgment and mistakes were not over after this breakfast meeting with Christ. The Shepherd knew that, and entrusted him with his sheep anyway.

Practice resurrection, we are told, with no thought of being perfect—or successful.

Clarence Jordan practiced resurrection by forming a Christian community called Koinonia in Georgia during the 1940s and 50s. The community was open to people of all races in a time when the world around them was segregated. One night, the Ku Klux Klan visited the Koinonia farm and burned down all the buildings except the one in which Jordan and his wife and child lived. That building they riddled with gunshot. During the raid, Jordan recognized the voice of one of the hooded attackers: it belonged to a local newspaperman.

The next day, Jordan returned to the fields to hoe and plant, continuing the work to which he had been called. Out into the fields walked the reporter heard the night before. "Well, Jordan," he said, "I guess you'll be moving on now, after all this damage." To which Jordan made no reply, but continued to hoe and plant, hoe and plant.

"Well, Mr. Jordan," inquired the reporter, "What is your reaction to last night's incident?"

Jordan continued to hoe and plant, hoe and plant.

"Mr. Jordan, what do you think? You've worked here fourteen years and all you've built lies in ruins. What do you think now that all you've worked for has failed?"

At which Clarence Jordan stopped hoeing, looked that unmasked Klansman in the eye and said: "You just never have understood about us Christians. It's not about being successful. It's about being faithful." And he went back to hoeing and planting.

What are we Christians to do in the face of evil?

Look it squarely in the eye as people who have seen beyond it, keep on hoeing and planting, *practice* resurrection, until in God's time and by God's hand, we get it right.

Amen.

SUGGESTIONS FOR WORSHIP

Call to Worship (adapted from Psalm 30)

LEADER: Sing praises to the Lord, and give thanks to God's holy name:

PEOPLE: **For God's anger is but for a moment, and God's favor is for a lifetime!**

LEADER: God has turned our mourning into dancing and girded us with gladness!

PEOPLE: **O Lord our God, we will give thanks to Thee forever!**
[Organist breaks into "Blessing and Honor" (Horatius Bonar, 1866)]

Prayer of Confession

LEADER: Almighty God, before whom all creatures of land and sea and myriads of angels fall down in breathless praise, we join our voices in songs of blessing and honor to you. But we confess that while we praise you with our lips, our lives fall short of the glory of you, our God. And so, in humility, we keep silence before you now: in the silence, show us how we have disappointed you, that we might acknowledge our sin, and turn away from it. *(attentive silence)*

PEOPLE: **Lord, have mercy upon us, and make of us people worthy to be called your own.**

113

Assurance of Pardon

LEADER: Friends, in the resurrection of Jesus Christ, God has shown us that "God's anger is but for a moment, but God's favor is for a lifetime!" In Jesus Christ, God has wound us round with mercy. Friends, believe the good news:

PEOPLE: **In Jesus Christ, we are forgiven!**

Charge and Benediction

Let us go forth into the world as people of the resurrection,
people who can look evil in the eye and see beyond it
to the sure and certain day
when God at last shall turn all our mourning into dancing.
Let us go forth in the power of the Holy Spirit
and *practice* resurrection.
Let God's people say, "AMEN!"

Fourth Sunday of Easter

René Rodgers Jensen

Acts 9:36-43: Peter raises the widow Tabitha from the dead, demonstrating that Jesus' prophetic ministry continues in the community of faith.

Psalm 23: The best known psalm, possibly the best known passage of scripture in the Bible, it uses the imagery of God as the good shepherd who provides protection and guidance.

Revelation 7:9-17: The Lamb is the shepherd who dwells among the redeemed who have survived the great ordeal, guiding them to springs of living water.

John 10:22-30: Pressed to declare plainly whether or not he is the Messiah, Jesus responds by saying that he knows his sheep and they follow him.

REFLECTIONS

As I was preparing this sermon, the school shooting in Littleton, Colorado, occurred. Fifteen persons, including the two high school seniors who were identified as the shooters, were killed. Twenty-three were wounded, many seriously. Particularly disturbing were the reports of the apparent relish with which the two young gunmen mowed down their classmates.

What does the church, what does the Scripture, what does God have to say in the face of such human tragedy and human sin? These were the very difficult and painful questions that confronted me while preparing the sermon.

Providentially, the lectionary provided the perfect scripture with which to address at least some of those questions. The twenty-third psalm is possibly the best known passage of scripture in the entire

Bible. Before the Littleton tragedy, I had been puzzling over how to make this familiar passage seem fresh and new. After Littleton, the very familiarity of the psalm became a strength. The ancient, well-known words, which the congregation recited together from memory, became words of healing and hope.

A SERMON BRIEF

My new favorite book is *Traveling Mercies* by Anne Lamott. I like many things about this book—Lamott's unflinchingly honest, often funny, occasionally profane way of looking at her life and her faith. I like the way she talks about prayer as putting something in God's in-box and the way she explains why she makes her son Sam go to church (because she outweighs him by seventy-five pounds). And I particularly like the title of the book: *Traveling Mercies*. Traveling mercies is an old prayer from the African American community for a safe journey and a safe return home; Lamott uses it as a metaphor for the graces, mercies, and blessings, both great and small, that get us through this life.

The twenty-third psalm is about traveling mercies. God, the good shepherd, leads us to green pastures and beside still waters, guides us down the right path, feeds us, restores us, shelters us, looks after us, keeps us safe. Traveling mercies.

In a life that so often feels scary and dangerous, when disaster can lurk around any corner, it is no wonder that this psalm, this prayer, this hope for traveling mercies, is so loved. If most of us can quote any piece of scripture from memory, it is this psalm. In times of crisis, it is these six verses we turn to. So I was not surprised the morning after the horrific shooting at Columbine High School in Littleton, Colorado, to hear an interview with a fifteen-year-old girl outside the high school. She had brought two poster board cards to lay outside the school. One card said, "May God be with you." The other bore the hand printed words of the twenty-third psalm.

I don't know that young girl's name, but I do know that she was very wise. Because that week Littleton, Colorado, became the valley of the shadow of death.

Before that the valley of the shadow of death was Springfield, Oregon, and Jonesboro, Arkansas; Pearl, Mississippi, and Paducah, Kentucky. The valley of the shadow of death goes by many names. We have known it as Kosovo and Rwanda, Belfast and Beirut, Waco and Oklahoma City. The reality is that any place, every place, can become the valley of the shadow of death.

A Catholic priest in Littleton, leading a worship service just hours after the attack on the high school, somberly told the shocked and grieving persons gathered there, that "no place is safe." This week we have learned that hard lesson all over again. Any place can become the valley of the shadow of death.

Now we don't like to believe that. We want to believe that we are safe. Over and over, in Jonesboro and Pearl and Paducah and Springfield and Littleton, we have heard the same words, "This can't be happening here." And we here in our own community understand that disbelief. That high school could be here, in one of our comfortable suburban neighborhoods. Those kids, both the victims and the perpetrators, look like our kids. The pleasant homes and the nice cars look like our homes and our cars. These people, the grieving parents and the terrified students and the shell-shocked teachers, look like us. It could have been us. It could yet be us. Any place can become the valley of the shadow of death.

So we seek ways to make our lives safer, more secure. The home security business is booming. Gated communities are becoming more and more desirable places to live. We enroll in self-defense classes. We put metal detectors in high schools, and post security guards in strategic positions. We stash guns under our beds or in our night stands, or in the glove compartments of our cars. In so many ways, some common sense, some foolish, some dangerous, we seek to secure the safety of ourselves and those we love.

But the truth is, ultimately nothing can guarantee security. We cannot build our walls high enough, we cannot devise security systems sophisticated enough, we cannot carry guns big enough to guarantee that we and those we love will always be safe. Cars crash. Viruses invade the body. There are tornadoes and cancer and heart attacks, train wrecks and airplane crashes. Yes, and there are gunmen and muggers and drive-by shootings. The priest in Colorado was right. No place is safe.

So does that make this psalm just a mockery and a sham? Is the promise of green pastures and still waters, right paths and protection from enemies, is it all just a bunch of pretty words without much meaning or substance? It is. It is if we take the psalm as a written guarantee of safety and security, a promise of a lifetime supply of still waters and green pastures. If we think that this psalm means that God is promising us a life with no trouble, no problems, no rocky roads or rough waters, no pain or difficulty or hard times, no loss and no grief,

117

then this psalm is a lie. If we think believing in God and following Christ and going to church is another way of trying to keep ourselves safe, if we assume being a Christian works like some sort of spiritual security device protecting us from all harm, then we are deceiving ourselves. Because this psalm is not a promise of life without pain and difficulty. It is a promise of God's unending and unfailing presence.

Theologian Hans Kung says that "God's love does not protect us *against* suffering, but it protects us *in* all suffering." Even when we walk through the valley of the shadow of death, God is with us. Even there God comforts and sustains us. The twenty-third psalm is not a promise that we will never walk through the valley, but it is a promise that we will never walk through that valley alone.

Of the horrific accounts of what happened in Columbine High School, for me one of the most painful was the story that the killers taunted one of the girls, asking, "Do you believe in God?" She answered "yes" and then they killed her. Now some people may ask, even some among us, where was God at that moment? What good did it do that child to believe in God when she died anyway? Why didn't God stop that bullet and all the other bullets? Why didn't God keep this horror from happening? If God is good, how can such evil exist? Those are hard questions, but important ones. We shouldn't flinch from asking them. I don't have any pat or easy answers to any of those questions. But one thing I do know, that I believe with all my heart and soul and strength. I know that God was with that girl as she died. That God was with each of the fifteen when they died, even the two tormented teens who perpetrated the massacre.

Suzanne Wilson, whose daughter Brittany was among those killed in the school shooting in Jonesboro, Arkansas, a year earlier, was interviewed following the tragedy in Colorado. At the end of the interview she said that it was only by the grace of God that she had gotten through the last year, only by the grace of God that she was able to get through each day. I know that in a specific and painful way that is true of Suzanne Wilson, who has suffered the greatest loss that any parent can know. But it is also true for each of us. It is only by the grace of God that we get through each day.

This is the answer to our prayer for traveling mercies: that by the grace of God we get through each day. And that one way or another, God will see us safely home. Even though no place is safe, and any place can become the valley of the shadow of death, we are not alone. The God who walks with us will see us through even the valley of the shadow of death. No place is safe, yet for those who walk with God

118

any place can become a green pasture. I was so moved by how the area around Columbine High School became a carpet of flowers and prayers. It became a sacred place. Goodness vanquished evil and created holy ground out of a killing field. That's what is promised in this psalm. Even though no place is safe, with God every place is safe. God's goodness and mercy will follow us all the days of our lives, and we shall dwell in God's house forever.

SUGGESTIONS FOR WORSHIP

Call to Worship

LEADER: We come this morning from places of turbulence and difficulty.
PEOPLE: We come seeking green pastures and still waters.
LEADER: We come weary from stumbling down the wrong roads and encountering dead-ends.
PEOPLE: We come seeking the way.
LEADER: We come pursued by the enemies of despair, cynicism, and materialism.
PEOPLE: We come seeking goodness, mercy, and love.

Prayer of Confession

God of life and hope and possibility, we confess that often we are tempted by the wrong paths. We have taken the pathways that promise safety and security. Pathways with sign posts bearing the names of wealth, success, materialism, cynicism, and isolation. But these pathways have left us lost and weary, frightened and alone. Gentle Shepherd, you alone can lead us by the right paths. You alone can defeat our enemies. You alone can walk with us through the valley of the shadow of death. Teach us to walk with you alone as our guide and guardian. Amen.

Benediction

Now go forth knowing that whether your way takes you beside still waters, or along a bumpy road, or even into the valley of the shadow of death, God is with you.

Fifth Sunday of Easter

René Rodgers Jensen

Acts 11:1-18: The summary of the extended narrative in Acts 10, this story of the baptism of the Gentile Cornelius and his household marks a watershed in the life of the early church.

Psalm 148: An exuberant summons for all creation to join in praising God.

Revelation 21:1-6: John's eschatological vision, "a new heaven and a new earth," in which God dwells with humanity.

John 13:31-35: Jesus gives his disciples a new commandment, to love one another.

REFLECTIONS

For many years I disliked the book of Acts and disliked preaching from it. Two things changed my mind. One was William Willimon's excellent commentary on Acts for the Interpretation series. This commentary helped me make friends with Acts and understand its message as I never had before. In this sermon I am greatly indebted to Willimon and his insights.

The second thing that changed my mind was the realization that the story of the first church is a rich resource for the contemporary church, because the church at the turn of the millennium has much in common with the church of the first century. Both are struggling toward new ways of being faithful in a culture that is indifferent or even hostile to the gospel message. Both are struggling with questions of identity and mission. Nowhere is this more clear than in the story of the conversion of Cornelius and his household. And while we talk of Cornelius's conversion, we are also talking about the conversion of Peter and the leaders of the church. Both conversions are necessary in order for the gospel message to spread.

In this sermon I try to lay the experience of the early church along-side the experience of the contemporary church, and find those points where the experiences intersect. As always in preaching on texts that touch on the relationship between Judaism and Christianity, it is important to be sensitive not to stray into inadvertent, but nevertheless harmful, anti-Jewish ways of speaking of the Jewish faith.

A SERMON BRIEF

It is difficult for us, standing at a distance of two thousand years, to understand what the excitement was all about. So Peter had lunch with a few Gentile friends. What's the big deal? Let's take a few moments to try and understand just what issues the young Christian community of Peter's time was wrestling with.

Christians today often ask, "Will the Jews be saved?" Many, many times over my years as a pastor, laypersons have come to me with this question, or it has arisen in the midst of Bible study or a Sunday school class. This is the question of those of us who know God's love, and rest assured in the promise of salvation, deeply and lovingly concerned with those we fear do not have that assurance. It is the question we "insiders" ask of those we perceive to be "outsiders." But for the church of Peter's time, the question of who was saved and who was not, who was an insider and who was an outsider, was quite different. For the young Christian community at the time of the book of Acts, there was no question whether or not the Jews would be saved. God had called the Jews to be God's chosen people, and every act of God since then, from the call of Abraham to the birth of Christ, confirmed that call. So Peter passionately preached on the day of Pentecost to the Jews in Jerusalem, "For the promise is to you and to your children."

The question that hangs over the book of Acts, that propelled Paul's ministry, that preoccupied the young church was *not:* "Can the Jews be saved?" The pivotal question for the young Christian community was: "Can the *Gentiles* be saved?" Can these outsiders be brought within the circle of God's salvation?

It is important for us to remember that Christianity began as a sect within Judaism. Jesus was a Jew. All of the first twelve disciples were Jews. Those three thousand baptized on the day of Pentecost were Jews. All remained Jews, even after they became followers of Jesus.

They continued to worship in the temple or synagogue, and to be faithful to Jewish law, including Jewish dietary law. Paul, that great missionary to the Gentiles, wrote long after he became a follower of Jesus that he continued to faithfully observe Jewish law. So Peter, when he had this vision of the clean and unclean animals, protested his obedience to Jewish dietary law: "But Lord, I have never eaten anything profane or unclean."

So we see that in its earliest days, church was made up of Jewish Christians, followers of Christ who continued to be faithful to Jewish law and practice. But with the conversion of Cornelius and his household, this community of Jewish Christians had to wrestle with whether or not to welcome Gentile Christians into the community of faith. Can the outsiders become insiders?

Christians may have a difficult time understanding the relevance or importance of something like Jewish dietary law. William Willimon notes:

> Only these laws stood in the way of the assimilation (and thus, destruction) of Jews as Jews. They identified, demarcated faithfulness in the midst of incredible pressure to forsake the faith, drop one's particularities and become a good citizen of the [Roman] Empire. A little pork here, a pinch of incense to Caesar there, and it will not be long before the faith community will be politely obliterated. . . . The dietary laws are not a matter of etiquette or peculiar culinary habits. They are a matter of survival and identity for Jews.[1]

This crucial question of identity and survival is hanging over the young church when Peter receives the vision of clean and unclean animals that leads to the conversion of Cornelius and his household. This dramatic narrative, the longest in the book of Acts, sets the stage for all that follows in the book of Acts (and, we might even say, all that follows for the next two thousand years): Paul's mission to the Gentiles and the rapid expansion of the church throughout the Roman Empire.

When Peter receives his vision of the clean and unclean animals, God isn't asking him to forsake his faithful observance of Jewish dietary law. God *is* challenging Peter to widen and expand his understanding of the church's mission and purpose. When Peter witnesses the Holy Spirit falling upon Cornelius and all his household, he finally understands that God's mission is to everyone who would hear the good news!

So what does this story have to say to us? A lot, I think. The church at the turn of the millennium, like the church in the first century, is also struggling with questions of identity and survival. There are lots of experts who are predicting that within a hundred years or so, mainline churches will cease to exist. Like the church of the first century, we exist in a culture that is indifferent or even hostile to the core values of the gospel. Like the church of the first century, God is calling the church today to do a new thing, to struggle toward new and different ways of being a community and people of faith.

Like the early church, we are having to reach new understandings of what is clean and unclean, what is sacred and what is secular, who is an insider and who is an outsider in the life of the church. And, like the early church, we are discovering that we may have drawn our lines of what is clean and unclean, who are the insiders and who are the outsiders, much more narrowly that God draws those lines.

The flash points for these discussions are many. For some the issue is music and styles of worship. What kind of music, what style of worship, is appropriate and faithful to the gospel? For a long time, we in the church believed that one kind of music was acceptable for worship and all other kinds were not. Sometimes we have acted as if God personally made an eleventh commandment, specifying the kind of music allowed in worship. Organ music was church music, other kinds were not. Our preferences have divided us.

For others the issue is dress. What kind of clothes are acceptable to wear to worship? Many of us were taught as we grew up that honoring God means dressing with a certain degree of formality for worship. Yet, as a nation, we are becoming more and more casual in our dress. In many corporations—even some of the most conservative—casual clothes are now acceptable office wear. Inevitably this dress-down trend is also affecting the church.

Are we only going to accept people who are willing and able to dress up for church? If a person can only afford casual clothes, are they unacceptable in our church? Or is giving someone the opportunity to hear the gospel of Jesus Christ more important than what they wear? A few months ago I was commiserating with a friend who has teenage children on how difficult it is to get teenagers to dress up. She said, only half jokingly, "My kids and I have a deal. They aren't sexually active, and they can wear whatever they want to church." This mother thought the most important thing was to get her teenagers to church, even if they were wearing jeans. She figured that what counted was coming to church and Sunday school, hearing God's word and making Christian friends. And if to have that happen she had to compromise on what they wore, that was okay.

For some the tension is around who may be sitting beside us in worship. It has long been noted that Sunday morning at 11:00 is the most segregated hour in our country. How truly open are we to receiving persons of color into our church? What about persons with differing sexual orientation? What about the poor, the homeless, the outcast? How genuinely welcoming are we to each of these groups? Can we, like Peter, accept the possibility that the Holy Spirit can fall upon even these? Or do we have a visceral reaction of repulsion that whispers to us, "unclean"?

Imagine what would have happened to the early church if they had stuck to their narrow understanding of who and what was acceptable to God. What if Peter had stubbornly rejected the meaning of God's vision, and refused to associate with Gentiles, refused to believe that Gentiles could be saved? What if he had stubbornly clung to his narrow understanding of what and who was clean and unclean? If the early Jewish Christian leaders of the church had not followed God's leading, and embraced first Peter's and then Paul's mission to the Gentiles, there's good chance you and I wouldn't be here today. But by the grace of God, those early leaders did expand their vision, and because of that countless millions have been saved.

Now we face the same challenge. Can we expand our own understanding of what is clean and unclean, what is sacred and what is secular, what is acceptable to God and what is not? Do we have the courage and vision and capacity to grow in faith that characterized Peter and those other early leaders in the church? Can we come to understand that when it comes to spreading the good news, God truly has no partiality or prejudice about how it should be done, or who is worthy to receive the good news?

Good question.

SUGGESTIONS FOR WORSHIP

Call to Worship (based on Revelation 21:1-6)

LEADER: Then I saw a new heaven and a new earth;
PEOPLE: **For the first heaven and the first earth had passed away.**
LEADER: A voice from heaven proclaimed: See the dwelling of God is with all humanity.
PEOPLE: **God will dwell with us, and we will be God's people.**

LEADER: God will wipe every tear from our eyes.
PEOPLE: **Death will be no more; mourning and crying and pain will be no more.**
LEADER: God is the Alpha and the Omega, the beginning and the end. God makes all things new.

Prayer of Confession

God of new things, forgive us when we try to make the new heaven and the new earth look like the old. Gently guide us when we try to make the ways of the present and the future conform to the norms of the past. Shake us with the ongoing power of your Spirit, which constantly creates and re-creates. You understand why we cling so tenaciously to the status quo. Help us to understand why we must let go.

Assurance of Pardon

Believe the good news!
Those who are in Christ are new creations.
The old has passed away. Behold! The new has come!

Benediction

Now go forth in love, for it is by our love for one another, our love for the whole world, that the world will know us as followers of Christ.

1. William Willimon, *Acts. Interpretation: A Bible Commentary for Teaching and Preaching* (Atlanta: John Knox Press, 1988), p. 96.

Sixth Sunday of Easter

Barbara Cawthorne Crafton

Acts 16:9-15: Paul journeys to Macedonia, having had a vision convincing him that God is calling him to preach there. He speaks with a group of women in Philippi. Lydia, a wealthy cloth merchant, listens, believes, and is baptized with her household. She invites Paul and his company to lodge with her during their stay.

Revelation 21:10; 22–22:5: There will come a time when God's glory will be unchallenged. In a heavenly city of God, the glory of God will give light. All therein will see and worship God face to face.

Psalm 67: A psalm of praise, looking toward the spread of God's dominion throughout all the nations.

John 14:23-29: Jesus, preparing to leave his disciples, leaves them his peace. It is not like the peace the world gives. It provides us with the ongoing presence of the spirit of Christ, even though we experience the absence of the earthly Jesus of Nazareth.

REFLECTIONS

How will we continue our life in Christ when Jesus is no longer standing before us? This was a fearful question for the disciples, who had not yet experienced themselves as a church, but as a band of followers very dependent upon their Lord. It's the same question we all have to ask ourselves, though. We don't have access to Jesus of Nazareth in person. How will we connect with God in the midst of our lives here on the earth? The church really didn't grow large during the earthly ministry of Jesus. It was later, when his physical body was no longer around, that the church was filled with the Spirit that enabled it to grow and spread throughout the world.

Christians often say they wish they'd been alive when Jesus was. Surely they would never be troubled by doubt if they could actually see and hear him! But many people saw and heard Jesus and did not believe—enough of them so that he could be arrested, tried, and killed in the space of a few days without anybody making much of a fuss at all. We are not farther from him because we do not share a historical era with the historical Jesus. The Spirit is within us, vividly present in the church. And nothing has been lost.

A SERMON BRIEF

I was driving home from a retreat with another woman I didn't know very well. We chatted the miles away as people do on car trips: children, husbands, histories. "I feel I'm in a pretty good place these days," she said as she drove. "I mean, as long as I have my husband, I'm okay."

Wow, I thought. That didn't sound like a very good place to me at all. It sounded pretty precarious. The life of one person stands between you and chaos? Sooner or later, you won't *have* your husband. He will die, or you will. Whichever it is, you are absolutely certain to be parted.

Everything and everyone we love is in that category: we will lose them all. Without exception. It's not a matter of *if*, but *when*. We will all lose everything.

When Jesus told his disciples about the peace he left with them, he knew that he was going to leave them. He knew, too, that they had no idea of how they would manage without him. He knew that they thought his physical presence was necessary to their spiritual well-being, and that they were about to lose that presence.

We know all about that. Have you lost someone you loved? Wasn't the sense of that dear one's absence all you knew in those first days and weeks? Didn't those days pass in a blur of exhaustion and grief, and didn't you wonder at times how on earth you were going to go on?

The process of regaining the presence of the beloved dead in another way is a gradual one, in my experience. It just doesn't happen in a week or two. But, as time goes by, the life that was lived before and the life that is lived now come to look more clearly like *one* life, a life that is changed, not ended. Do I wish I could call my mom on the phone and talk the way we used to? You bet. But don't

127

I also feel her love with me all the time, a love that formed me and trained me and still stands by me? I can't explain it, but neither can I deny it. Somehow, she is still here. And so is my dad. And my brother, and the saints from generations past. More than just a memory. A presence.

For centuries, Christians have tried to understand the life that continues beyond the boundaries of this one. They have often done so in very limited ways. Many have wanted to limit it to believers or to people who have behaved themselves, as if God's great love were constrained by the barriers we erect against one another, as if God's love was no match for our sinfulness, as if God were incapable of acting except in the ways God has already acted with us, as if our reality is the only possible one. So there were a few interesting theological developments along the way: the medieval doctrine of limbo, for example, in which the unbaptized hung suspended for eternity, not punished, but certainly not rewarded. And purgatory, in which your sins could be paid off in time, and then you could enter Paradise.

They made a certain sense, these complicated inventions. But when we are talking about life in the Spirit, *making sense* is not of paramount importance. Life in the Spirit doesn't *make sense*. Only life on earth makes sense, for that's what making sense is: conforming to the way things are in the world. But life in the Spirit is not limited by the way things are here. The Spirit of Christ encompasses this world, but is not limited by it. There is a lot we don't know. A lot that just won't make sense. You'll miss your dear one mightily when he or she dies, because your world will have a hole ripped right through it. Missing him or her makes sense. But your spirit, biding its time, waiting and looking and listening for the things of God, will begin to feel the comfort only the Spirit can give. A comfort that makes no sense at all. A comfort that can't be described very well in words at all, because it comes from a reality beyond human words.

The disciples didn't understand that they were the church, not at first. They didn't experience the comfort the Spirit offers every minute of every day for the rest of their lives. They dropped the ball sometimes, just as we do. They were honest enough to describe it for us in the Scriptures: we can read about it, we can *see* them behaving rather badly sometimes, just as we sometimes behave rather badly. Their spiritual selves were sometimes undermined by their humanness, as ours sometimes are. The Spirit was always present with them, but they didn't always get it, just as we do not always get it. The Spirit is with us always, but its peace is not the peace the world gives. And we live in the world. We stand uncomfortably, sometimes, with one foot on earth and one in heaven.

And God knows this about us. And loves us through it. And heals us. And we are not alone.

SUGGESTIONS FOR WORSHIP

Call to Worship

LEADER: Rejoice, all you who love our God.
PEOPLE: And keep God's word.
LEADER: Rejoice, all you who love our God.
PEOPLE: For Jesus has returned to the Creator.
LEADER: Rejoice, all you who love our God.
PEOPLE: For the Spirit lives among us and strengthens us.

Prayer of Confession

O God, you know that we cannot lay hold of our experience of your Spirit and keep it. You know that it often slips from our grasp, and we forget that you are always with us. You know that we sometimes live as if we did not have the peace of Christ with us. Remind us, O God, who we are and whose we are, and build in us the awareness of what we know to be true: that your Spirit is with us always, even to the end of the age. Amen.

Words of Assurance

Even though you forget God, God does not forget you. Even when you lose sight of God, God sees you. Even when you are tempted to despair, God will lift you up and restore you to perfect peace.

Benediction

May God, who created us out of love and sustains us in love, guide you in the love of Christ, this day and always. Amen.

Ascension Day

Barbara Cawthorne Crafton

Acts 1:1-11: This first chapter of the account of what life was like in the earliest church begins with a statement about the many proofs, experienced by witnesses, that Jesus was indeed alive, and continues with an account of the Ascension: "he was lifted up, and a cloud took him out of their sight."

Psalm 47 or Psalm 93: Two psalms are appointed. Psalm 47 was probably first used as a praise song in temple worship celebrating the reign of God over all the nations, not just the children of Israel. Psalm 93 is similar; it celebrates the rule over the natural order. In each case, we sing of a God not confined to any political or ethnic part of the world, but a God who unites all in holiness.

Ephesians 1:15-23: Christ has been exalted over all creation, transcending all human divisions and all human powers: "the fullness of the one who fills all in all."

Luke 24:44-53: Jesus speaks of the fulfillment of Moses, the prophets and the psalms which he represents, and opens the minds of his disciples to understand the Scriptures. They are to be witnesses to that fulfillment. Then he is taken up into heaven, and the disciples return to Jerusalem "with great joy."

REFLECTIONS

At first, the disciples had enough on their plates just coming to terms with the resurrection in their own lives. Soon, they would need to begin to deal with how their powerful experience related to their experiences as Jews. The dominion of Christ over the whole of creation and the universalizing implications of that rule—primarily, that Christ is for the whole world, not just for the children of Israel—was not immediately obvious to people raised with a powerful sense of Israel's uniqueness and a strong need to defend it against outside domination. The Ascension certifies that the whole Christ event transcends what we know about the way things work. Whatever else Jesus is, it is not just business as usual. In a sense, all bets are off: your nationality, your training, your status, your powers of deduction, none of these accomplish for you what Jesus Christ has accomplished. And so we are a new creation.

A SERMON BRIEF

Packing up my father's library after he died, I found several books about the Shroud of Turin. I remember that he was fascinated by the famous long strip of cloth, said to be the cloth in which Jesus' body was wrapped after the crucifixion, bearing the imprint of the dead face of the Messiah himself. There were also a few books about life after death, books featuring interviews with people who had been resuscitated on the operating table. And, I recall, one book called *Who Moved the Stone?* whose premise was that the resurrection must have been real because the stone would have been too heavy for anyone to move.

The Gospel writers, too, thought the stone significant, which was why they included it in their recounting of the events leading to the resurrection. They wanted to be sure we understood it was a physical event; they wanted to give us the evidence they had that the resurrection was real.

My dad shared their interest in the physical: he'd get curious about something and read everything he could get his hands on. He was a lawyer, as well as a clergyman, and what he loved was evidence. He loved certainty. That long ago event that has so shaped us—he wanted to understand it completely. He wanted proof.

I think we understand that impulse. Who doesn't want to understand? Who doesn't want proof? It is what sets us apart from the animals—our ability to analyze. We don't lose that part of ourselves when we become Christians. But we certainly change our relationship to it, for so much of faith rests on things that can never be understood or proved.

And so the Ascension of our Lord has turned out to be a useful thing in this regard. It clears up some problems of evidence with which the resurrection plagues us. Throughout the narratives of the

Easter season, we have encountered the work of early Christian spin doctors more than once. I think, for instance, of the careful and rather stagey report in Matthew 28, detailing a scheme among the chief priests and the elders after the crucifixion.

> Some of the guard went into the city and told the chief priests everything that had happened. After the priests had assembled with the elders, they devised a plan to give a large sum of money to the soldiers, telling them, "You must say, 'His disciples came by night and stole him away while we were asleep.' If this comes to the governor's ears, we will satisfy him and keep you out of trouble." So they took the money and did as they were directed. And this story is still told among the Jews to this day. (Matthew 28:11-15)

And of their earlier conversation with Pilate:

> Sir, we remember what that imposter said while he was still alive, "After three days I will rise again." Therefore command the tomb to be made secure until the third day; otherwise his disciples may go and steal him away, and tell the people, "He has been raised from the dead," and the last deception would be worse than the first. (Matthew 27:63-64)

Clearly, Matthew brings this up because *other* people were bringing it up. People didn't believe Jesus had risen from the dead. Who can blame them? Would we believe such a thing just because someone told us it had happened? I don't know why we would; nothing in our experience tells us that people can rise from the dead. Surely these little asides are included for our benefit. Not only were the Jews expressing doubts about the resurrection, Christians had them, too.

The Ascension ministers to a very practical problem about the resurrection: if Jesus has been raised, then where is he? Why don't we see him walking around anywhere? We know he wasn't raised just to grow old and then die again, like poor Lazarus must have had to do. Some explanation must be provided, some means of getting a risen Christ out of town if people were going to continue to believe. The Ascension provides it: we stand openmouthed with the disciples and watch as Jesus is carried off into the sky. In some medieval paintings, we see his feet sticking out of the bottom of a cloud as he goes.

Who is to say what the risen Christ was like in the weeks immediately following the resurrection? No one now living can pretend to know. Whatever those witnesses experienced translates poorly to the written page. Words come up wanting in their attempts to describe it. We slam quickly into brick walls of contradiction, needing to come up with explanations we cannot possibly provide. So we are shown a Jesus eating fish. We see him wafting through a wall to proffer a wounded hand for our inspection. We are shown a Jesus who seems solid but then disappears, a Jesus strangely unrecognizable to people who have known him for years.

All of this is by way of a reminder, in case we needed one, that the resurrection has nothing to do with the laws of earthly existence as we know it. And that hitting it with a sledgehammer until it fits the way things work here on earth will do little to advance our understanding of it. And that "understanding" is probably not the operative word here. As natural an impulse as it is with us, we're going to have to abandon our usual method of discovery and understanding when it comes to dealing with the risen Christ. Theorizing about the biochemistry of what went on in the wee hours of that blessed Easter morning won't get us far, either. The Shroud of Turin attracts that part of us that hopes to understand and, because we understand it, to control. But we will never understand God, and it is certain that we will never control God.

I smiled as I thumbed through the book on the Shroud and read my dad's earnest marginal notes. I smiled, and I missed him. He was really trying to understand. That was so like him. He died, of course, as all of us die, *not* understanding. But he *knows* now, knows all about it. As we will all one day know, all of us, when we are in Christ and Christ is all in all.

SUGGESTIONS FOR WORSHIP

Call to Worship

LEADER: Where now is your God?
PEOPLE: **God has gone up with a shout.**
LEADER: Where now is your God?
PEOPLE: **Jesus was lifted up, and a cloud took him out of our sight.**
LEADER: Where now is your God?
PEOPLE: **Far above all rule and authority and power and dominion, and above every name that is named, not only in this age, but in the age to come.**
LEADER: And the church is Christ's body, the fullness of Christ who fills all in all.

Opening Prayer

Most gracious God, in you we find the courage to stretch beyond our old ways of knowing and of being known. Give us the knowledge of your resurrection in our own lives, a truth we cannot deduce but must experience. Nurture in us that sense that sees you in all things, and fill us with the power to give that sight to all who long for it. In the name of the risen and ascended Christ, we ask it. Amen.

Prayer of Confession

Gracious God, we struggle to understand your presence in our lives. Over and over we find ourselves limited in believing in you by the limits that bind us. We forget that you are mightier than we are, that your ways are not our ways, that the resurrected life is not like this life. Lead us through our limitations into your truth, so that one day we will see and know, as you see and know us. Amen.

Assurance of Pardon

Our God, whose only begotten One lived our life and died our death, has raised Jesus to glory so that we might follow. Be of good cheer: you will live in the fullness of God, and Christ will be all in all.

Benediction

May God, who leads us into the truth, illumine our understanding and fill us with the power of the Holy Spirit. Amen.

Seventh Sunday of Easter

Melinda Contreras-Byrd

Acts 16:16-34: Proclaiming God's new word in God's new way results in Paul and Silas's imprisonment, which serves to accomplish God's miraculous work of salvation and reconciliation.

Psalm 97: Our God reigns above all powers, working to bring vindication and justice to those who are righteous.

Revelation 22:12-14, 16-17, 20-21: The one who is Alpha and Omega promises a final return to reward those who have lived on earth in accord with God's ways.

John 17:20-26: Jesus' prayer for all his followers is that we will be able to demonstrate a love which will unify us with each other and with God.

REFLECTIONS

"All God's children got to cry sometimes" proclaims an old black proverb to the children of each successive generation. The questions are spoken aloud, "How can the innocent suffer?" "Why are the righteous oppressed?" "Where is the justice when exploitation seemingly reigns?" "Where is God in the midst of life's chaos?" Perhaps our greatest fear is that God has left us, or that we have diminished God's love for us, or that evil is in fact in charge.

As the Scriptures testify to the reality of suffering and hardship in the life of the believer, they also testify to the truth of God's promise to work all things together for good to those who love the Lord. What a blessing to realize that God is in charge, working in the lives of believers to bring about unity and reconciliation. The triumph of the Christian faith is repeated in Psalm 97. Praise God that although we cannot answer the questions of why the righteous suffer, we do have a response. Our response to trials and tribulations is made in an affirmation through tears that "[The Lord] guards the lives of the faithful; rescuing them from the hand of the wicked. . . . Light dawns for the righteous, and joy for the upright in heart" (Psalm 97:10*b*, 11*a*, paraphrase).

A SERMON BRIEF

The world is full of all kinds of people. We differ in gender and create sexism. We differ in race and create racism. Our attempts at unity create bigotry at worst and exclusive social clubs and civic organizations at best. We struggle in our loneliness, creating forms of togetherness that hinder, hurt, and destroy. Parents cling to their children refusing them the freedom to grow and mature. Men undercut women's sense of competence and self-worth. Women question men's ability to be sensitive, responsible, and nonviolent human beings. The people who are not like us will not conform, and their justified desire to maintain their individuality sometimes takes forms which separate them from us and from God. We band together to demonstrate whom we are *with* and whom we stand *against.* We attack. We imprison. We enslave. We exploit. We place in special classes. We categorize. We wage war. We kill.

Our attempts to cope and create a society that meets our needs have given us some of the most wonderful inventions, the most life-saving scientific breakthroughs, the most inventive and intriguing artistic expressions. Yet we have fashioned for ourselves a world which inspires both our awe and our terror!

My seven-year-old comes to me excitedly. Opening her small, outstretched hand, she peers up at me expectantly with her big, innocent, brown eyes. "Mommy, do I have enough for an ice cream?" she asks, with complete trust in my ability and willingness to help her do what she is unable to do. I count her money, explaining to her that she has extra money. She giggles at the thought that she has enough to buy ice cream and something more as well. I drop the counted money into her small brown hand, and without a thought she gallops off happily to make her purchase.

Yet something about her innocent round face and large trusting eyes makes me want to hold her to myself, to protect her and do everything within my power to keep her safe. I know that Alexa would extend her hand to anyone who is older, with the expectation that because they *could,* they *would* help. I also know with sadness that there are those who would take her money. There are those who would refuse to help her because her small hand is brown, and those who would fail to see the beauty and innocence that I see in her eyes. The heartbreaking thing about our world is that we live in it with those who would harm even someone who, in complete faith, trusted them with her little toy.

What tremendous love and joy even the faces of her children bring to this mother. What a blessing to discover that in keeping with the mother side of God, Jesus prays his high priestly prayer in John 17, committing these whom he has loved so much back into the hands of their loving Creator. As I pray for safety for my children, Kamaria and Alexa, Jesus prays for what is most needful to those who will follow him. He prays for an indwelling of God's Spirit in their lives, which will result in a participation in the very unity experienced in the Godhead.

For those who could be lost and swallowed up by the chaos of this world, Jesus-God prays in love. Within a world which needs a Megan Law, a holocaust remembrance day, civil rights laws, and a gay pride parade, Jesus sees his church as I see my children, and loves them.

What is the role and meaning of love and unity in a world in which the weak, powerless, and innocent are despised and exploited rather than loved and protected? Acts 16 relates that Paul and Silas came upon a young girl enslaved by an evil spirit. They had compassion for her and freed her from her life of torment. But, we are also told that others had come upon her before the disciples, and seeing her condition used it as a means for personal gain. Rather than rejoice over the possessed girl's healing, they were infuriated by their loss of income!

Paul and Silas were beaten and imprisoned for their righteous deed. Yet the Scripture tells us that their spirits remained strong and rather than protest, lament, or holler they prayed and sang songs of praise to the most high God. In the midst of an unjust world they stood as righteous witnesses to the existence of "a more excellent way." The miraculous happened, as Psalm 97 promised it would.

Appearances to the contrary notwithstanding, God is still on the throne. God's Spirit is moving in our world to call forth those who will stand for righteousness. God is preparing a day when justice will tower above injustice and the silence of peace will drown out the noise of war. God is preparing a day when the lives of the innocent taken senselessly will be given redemptive meaning by the hand of the Almighty. If not today, one day. If not today, one day there will be no more weeping in Ramah, and, praise God, Rachel *will* be comforted.

SUGGESTIONS FOR WORSHIP

Call to Worship

LEADER: Come let us rejoice and give thanks for our God is a Triune God, creator and sustainer of all life.

PEOPLE: **With one voice let us praise Yahweh's name.**

LEADER: We are graciously kept by God's sanctifying Spirit.

PEOPLE: **With one voice let us praise the Spirit of God.**

LEADER: We are redeemed and reconciled by the work of Jesus.

PEOPLE: **With one voice let us praise Jesus the Christ.**

LEADER: In the world we are ever in God's care. In God's time we are moving toward unity.

ALL: **So that with one true voice we can praise God's holy name.**

Prayer of Confession

O most holy and righteous God, our Creator, we are ever thankful for your loving presence in our world. We acknowledge that it is your grace that sustains us, your love that transforms us, your strength that draws us to you and to each other. We confess, our God, that we have not stood for justice. We have not struggled for peace. We have not walked in love and unity with all of your creation. Transform us, renew us, stir us up this day. Fix us, O mighty God, that we may be one in will, in spirit, in word, and in truth.

Words of Assurance

The word of God records Jesus' high priestly prayer. And so we stand today blessed. For Jesus Christ, our high priest, has prayed for us, placing us in the care of God our Creator. Through the grace of God we are forgiven, unified, empowered, and sent out to change our world.

Benediction

And now may our God who loves and redeems us, so fill your life with holy presence that you can sing songs of praise from the prisons of this life, and stand rejoicing as the earth shakes and the walls come tumbling down.

Pentecost Sunday

Mary Emaline Kraus

Psalm 104:24-34, 35*b*: The wonders of God are extolled. God's spirit is the source of creation, but when God's breath is taken away, death ensues.

Romans 8:14-17: Those who are led by the Spirit of God receive a spirit of adoption and are called children of God.

Acts 2:1-21: The Holy Spirit, represented by tongues of fire, descends upon a multicultural, multilingual community gathered on the day of Pentecost.

John 14:8-17 (25-27): Jesus promises the disciples that God will send an advocate—the spirit of truth—to be with them forever.

REFLECTIONS

Today we celebrate Pentecost, the coming of the Holy Spirit upon that diverse group of persons gathered in Jerusalem. We recognize Pentecost as the birthday of the church. The Gospel lesson foreshadows this event and the Romans text celebrates that those who follow the Spirit of God are God's adopted children and heirs.

The focus of today's service however, is on the text from Acts—that one unique moment in Christian history when the story of Babel is reversed. At Babel, those once united by language were dispersed to the various parts of the world, confused now by many languages that separated them. But at Pentecost, those once separated are now united—not under one culture and one language—but united by the power of the Holy Spirit, a power that allowed the multicultural, multilingual community to understand one another.

Pentecost is about experiencing the Holy Spirit's presence in our lives, about breaking down barriers that separate us, about being vehicles of God's Spirit for the world. "Your sons and your daughters shall prophesy, and your young men shall see visions, and your old men shall dream dreams" (Acts 2:17*b*).

There are many avenues in which a sermon on Pentecost could be developed. This particular sermon plays on a metaphor from Diana Eck's book *Encountering God:* "Holy Spirit holes."

A SERMON BRIEF

Go back with me in time, to a time before Gutenberg invented the printing press making it possible to put the stories of our faith into a book that could now be read by everyone. Go back with me to a time when people simply told the stories passed down from generation to generation.

In the centuries after the old Roman Empire fell and before Europe established itself as the new intellectual center, we have what is known as those Middle Ages. Now those of you who like history know that this time is often imaged as a period of cold weather, bad food, and nonexistent plumbing. This period was even called the Dark Ages.

But there was one bright spot in the darkness where medieval men and women from miles around could gather for comfort, care, and discipleship training. That place was the local cathedral. How ironic that these so-called Dark Ages are known for their stained glass windows. In actuality, our medieval forebears had a Bible but it wasn't a book, it was the cathedral itself. Here the paintings, the murals, the sculptures, the icons, the stained glass windows, the painted domes, the drama and the pageantry and the Eucharist all told stories of the faith.

Yet cathedrals were even more than massive open Bibles. They also acted as centers of community life: the courthouse for local lawmakers and keepers, a place where weary travelers could expect to find a meal and a safe place to sleep. The presence of a large, busy cathedral in any village guaranteed the community a more stable economic base and greater educational opportunities.

None of this even considers the main function of a cathedral as the center for religious life and worship, the work of caring for the souls in its community. In those days, religious faith was not a mere convenience or habit, it was the main support system in the lives of struggling, frightened, powerless women and men. The cathedral offered comfort, beauty, and security for all who entered the door.

Harvard scholar Diana Eck, in her book *Encountering God,* reveals some surprising aspects of religion in the medieval church. In those days, the liturgical calendar with its different seasons of the year, different colors, and special days shaped the daily lives of the people in those villages. Festivals, saints' days, holy days were all lived and breathed in their world. Professor Eck discovered that Pentecost was one of the most unique and creatively celebrated days.

In tenth-century Rome, for example, the church really knew how to throw its own birthday party in order to make the coming of the Holy Spirit a dramatic, dynamic event for the congregation. Pentecost involved architecture, not just anthems.

The custom of painting heavenly scenes on the great domes served not only to inspire devotion but also to disguise some discreet trap doors. These small openings were drilled through the roof and during the Pentecost worship service, some daring person would climb up on the roof and at the appropriate moment during the liturgy would release live doves through these holes.

Can you imagine looking up at a beautifully painted dome and all of a sudden, seeing these swooping, diving symbols of a vitally present Holy Spirit descending toward you below? At the same time, the choir would break into the whooshing and drumming sound of a holy windstorm!

Finally, as the doves were flying and the winds rushing, the ceiling holes would once again be utilized as bushels of rose petals were showered down on the congregation. These red, flickering bits of flowers symbolized tongues of flame falling upon all who waited below in faith.

These openings to the sky in medieval churches were called "Holy Spirit holes." Let's play with this image for a moment—"Holy Spirit holes. . ." Do we need a Holy Spirit hole to open us outward and skyward to the Divine?

Diana Eck believes we do. She writes:

> We need these Holy Spirit holes. Our churches need these skyward openings to the windrush of God, even the pentecostal churches that summon the Spirit every Sunday morning. Holy Spirit holes would be perpetual reminders to both the prophetic and the pentecostal movements in our churches that our knowledge of God is not complete. They would ceaselessly remind us that no image or icon, no petal or flame can domesticate God's Spirit. Its symbolic images, like the dove and the wildfire, are images of utter freedom.[1]

We might want to ask ourselves: have we created around ourselves a spiritual vacuum that allows no breath of wind to blow, instead of experiencing doves and flames swooping out from Holy Spirit holes? Have we insulated our souls from any surprise visitation?

Pentecost calls us to open ourselves to the wind. It is the wind-like quality of the Spirit that surprises us. . . . that takes us where we don't want to go . . . that is unpredictable . . . that drives us toward stillness . . . that drives us toward wholeness . . . that drives us toward shelter and safety.

Are there any Holy Spirit holes open in our ceiling here? In your home? In your work place? Your car? Your school? Are you willing this morning to become a Holy Spirit hole to those around you?

Let's sing a prayer to this end: (to the tune TRURO)

Blow Holy Spirit, Breath of Power
Send peace to give us strength to live this hour
O Breath of God, empower us to be
The folk of faith now joined in unity.[2]

Blow Holy Spirit where you will. Fill the earth. Let the breath of the Spirit blow in you and me. Blow Holy Spirit holes, blow. Let God's Spirit breathe through you and me. Amen!

SUGGESTIONS FOR WORSHIP

Call to Worship

LEADER: The day of Pentecost has come and we are together. Let us face bravely into the winds of God.

PEOPLE: **Surely God is in this place! The works of God surround us . . . listen . . . look!**

LEADER: The Spirit of God fills us with amazement. God sets us afire with wonder and awe.

PEOPLE: **We will sing to God as long as we live; we will celebrate the gifts of God.**

Prayer of Confession (in unison)

God of majesty and power, we tremble when we become aware of who you are. Who are we that you should visit us or expect something from us? We confess our preference for the predictable. We admit our resistance to your Spirit. We acknowledge our misuse of your gifts to us. We prefer our divisions to your unity. Forgive us, O God of power and might, that we may forgive. Draw us back into a right relationship with you, and with one another. Amen.

Words of Assurance

God has reached out to us once again, offering salvation, making us whole, drawing us into community where life is integrated and filled with meaning. The Spirit comes to us, making holy the commonplace. We are forgiven.

Benediction

There are in our day, many people who "cannot find God." I tell you: that God is in our future calling us; that God is in our past forgiving us; that God is in the present loving us. There is no greater blessing. Go in peace to be a Holy Spirit hole for those seeking God. Amen.

1. Diana Eck, *Encountering God: A Spiritual Journey from Bozeman to Banaras* (Boston: Beacon Press, 1993), p. 130.
2. This was an original composition prepared for the congregation to sing on Pentecost.

Ordinary Time 21 or Proper 16

Lynda Weaver-Williams

Jeremiah 1:4-10: For the prophet, the experience of divine call is intensely personal, molded into his being, even as Israel had been formed as God's treasured possession. Jeremiah's life is to be intertwined around this double helix of personal and public faith.

Psalm 71:1-6: This psalm of lament voices the dual message of complaint and trust, of keeping faith even while seemingly losing ground. The first six verses offer the psalmist's testimony of hope rooted in, once again, divine companionship from birth.

Hebrews 12:18-29: Contrasting the terrifying presence of God at Mt. Sinai with the accessibility of God through Jesus ("the mediator of a new covenant") via Mt. Zion, the writer reassures believers of God's "unshakable" presence.

Luke 13:10-17: This text offers the healing of a woman who cannot fully straighten herself and the story itself is encircled by a Sabbath dispute. It is often paired with the Luke 14:1-6 narrative in which Jesus pulls off another healing, this time of a man with dropsy; it also has the context of Sabbath controversy. This juxtaposition places a woman who is shrunken in size and cannot "right" herself alongside a man who is so full of himself, so swollen with his own fluids, that he too, is disabled. The good news is not simply that they each find healing, but that the system which victimized them both is challenged.

REFLECTIONS

The Gospel text finds Jesus once again in trouble; this time it is a Sabbath controversy. But as always, this "controversy" pericope conceals a deeper human struggle. In this case, the context of the controversy is the question of healing on the Sabbath, but Jesus attaches physical healing to spiritual liberation and presents to readers the question of freedom as divine intention: "Ought not this woman . . . be set free from this bondage on the sabbath day?" (13:16).

Marcus Borg suggests that the central conflict in the ministry of Jesus was that of his distinctive social paradigm, which was in direct opposition to the dominant sociopolitical vision of first-century Judaism.[1] In this text Jesus chooses compassion for the woman over Sabbath protocol, thus challenging the religious, social, and political world view of the synagogue.

The reminder for us all is that the accent of divine activity is always on the creation of new possibilities. God's strongest impulse is that of creating new life. In this narrative new possibilities emerge between the cracks of the old system, leaving everyone in the story—the woman, who is not named, the synagogue leader, and all listeners, including us—with questions as to where this divine dissonance, this unexpected freedom, will show up next!

A SERMON BRIEF

I have to confess: I am a pushover for beginnings. I like to visit newborns in the hospital; I like the smell of new paint in the hall of a school building preparing for students in the fall; I like groundbreaking ceremonies, the launching of new ships, and weddings. I like beginnings, and that is why in 1992, on a cold January 20, I found myself standing on the mall in Washington, D.C., listening to Maya Angelou offer her poem "On the Pulse of Morning": a gift of welcome for a new administration. Her voice sang out among the crowd, declaring that this moment was indeed the "pulse of a new day." She beckoned us to enter that moment, by looking "into your sister's eyes, And into your brother's face, Your country" and to speak a simple greeting, "with hope—Good morning."[2]

And I was lost in the moment of believing all over again in new possibilities. Now some years hence and several scandals later I do not regret that infatuation with the new. I am glad I can find such in this world where the Teacher claims "there is nothing new under the sun." It is that human inclination toward the new that brings us to this Gospel story of a new moment in the life of a woman who knew little of such possibilities—a moment brought to us courtesy of Jesus.

145

Don't miss the setup of this story: Jesus is teaching in the synagogue on the Sabbath. In other words, Jesus is doing the right thing in the right place at the right time. But not for long. He notices a woman. She doesn't approach him; she doesn't intrude; she acts with propriety. After all, she, too, is doing the right thing as best she can. As a woman in a restrictive religious context, she has limited options when it comes to religious activities. In some ways, things haven't changed much in twenty centuries, have they?

But Jesus notices her, speaks to her; he seems to have no hesitations about her. Even with first century Jewish protocol, Jesus doesn't miss a beat. He offers to her a freedom word: "Woman you are set free from your ailment!" A freedom word if ever there was one. Woman, you are free; you are released from whatever has held you down. Woman, you can stand up full and free in the grace of God. No more staring at feet; stand up and look us in the eye!

The word from Jesus on that day in the synagogue was to lighten the load, to let go and let God free us from whatever it is that has kept us bent over. The question of the nature of this woman's particular medical ailment leads us to our wrestling with our own particular ailment that has us bent double, that has kept us from standing full and free in the light of God.

In *Teaching a Stone to Talk,* Annie Dillard tells the story of the Franklin expedition, launched in 1845 to find a northwest passage across the high Canadian Arctic to the Pacific Ocean.[3] It was an elegant beginning: fine English china and sterling silver flatware for the officers and men, silk scarves, crystal goblets, a pump organ, and instead of extra fuel, a twelve-hundred volume library all stowed aboard two worthy vessels. Of course, the explorers were lost, all one hundred thirty-eight of them. For years the Inuit natives of the region happened across various nightmarish "tableaux" of members of the expedition who had set out across the ice pack for help. They had died on the ice with their silk scarves around their necks and their backpacks stuffed with sterling silver flatware. Proper items for English gentlemen, yes, but absolutely useless for an Arctic journey.

All of us are carrying such useless items; every one of us is hauling around some sterling silver flatware in our spiritual backpacks: heavy expectations of where we thought we'd be at age eighteen or thirty-five or fifty or sixty-two; the cumbersome baggage of how life is "supposed" to work out, how a marriage is supposed to be, what a family is supposed to look like, how we supposed our children would grow up. We have a double load of sterling silver flatware and, like the woman in the Gospel story, our burdens have us bent double.

Notice something about this story: Jesus didn't give this woman anything she didn't already have. He did not tell her she had great faith or that her sins were forgiven or that she had chosen wisely—things he did tell other women at other times in the Gospels. He simply empowered this woman to be what was in her to be. He gave her permission to stretch into her full being, but the raw material was already present: her bone and muscle and spine were set to do their intended work. Jesus gave her the password, the key, the power, the freedom word that enabled her new beginning in the world.

Notice something else about this story: there is a controversy over what happens, which, of course, seems to have been an everyday thing with Jesus in the Gospels. Not everyone believes in freedom, especially if we are talking about someone else's. There will always be people hanging around the synagogue, or around the church, who denounce any sign of grace. There will always be someone who gets bent out of shape when freedom breaks loose. There will always be someone to remind us of tradition, or the importance of unity, or the bottom line. There will always be someone who values protocol over people. We should not expect this freedom to be easy; it wasn't for Jesus and it won't be for his followers.

In her novel *Beloved* Toni Morrison's "unchurched" preacher woman, Baby Suggs, reminds her congregation of runaway slaves that freedom is organic: it is a living and breathing thing that they must lean toward, even in the moments when it is yet to be fully born. Every Saturday afternoon in a sacred, secret place in the woods she preaches to them the words of life:

> She told them that the only grace they could have was the grace they could imagine. That if they could not see it, they would not have it.
>
> "Here, she said, in this here place, we flesh; flesh that weeps, laughs; flesh that dances on bare feet in grass. Love it. Love it hard. Yonder they do not love your flesh. They despise it. *You* got to love it. This is flesh I'm talking about here. Flesh that needs to be loved. Feet that need to rest and to dance; backs that need support; shoulders that need arms, strong arms I'm telling you. And O my people, out yonder, hear me, they do not love your neck unnoosed and straight. And all your inside parts that they'd just as soon slop for hogs, you got to love them. The dark, dark liver—love it, love it, and the beat and beating heart, love that too. More than eyes or feet. More than your life-holding womb

and your life-giving private parts, hear me now, love your heart. For this is the prize."[4]

Sisters and brothers, let us love the prize, our God-given hearts, and let us attune ourselves to the freedom word of Jesus that will enable us to bring our whole beings—hesitant hearts, doubtful minds, bent backs, weary shoulders, straying feet, all of it—into the grace of this community we call church. Here, we can listen together for the divine word; here we can love the flesh that is so neglected; here we can support the shoulders that have carried burdens alone and here, we can help one another live into the freedom of this story: woman, man, child, friends; we are free from what holds us down. Let us live in the freedom of Christ.

SUGGESTIONS FOR WORSHIP

Call to Worship
(based upon Isaiah 43:16-21, New Jerusalem Bible)

LEADER: Thus says Yahweh, who made a way through the sea, a path in the raging waters; no need to remember past events, no need to think about what was done before.

PEOPLE: **Look, I am doing something new, now it emerges; can you not see it?**

LEADER: I am making a road in the desert and rivers in wastelands; the wild animals will honor me.

PEOPLE: **And my people, my chosen people whom I have shaped for myself, will broadcast my praises.**

Prayer of Confession

God who makes all things new, you call us into new life together as the church. Yet we struggle to be faithful, to receive Spirit, to live amid the new. Free us from the fear of the new things you are doing among us and stretch our vision to see beyond ourselves. Give us eyes to see, ears to hear, and hearts that burn with love for all creation.

148

Benediction

Send us out by your Spirit to embrace the new beginnings you have in store. Make us the glad, grateful, and fearless people of God.

1. Marcus Borg, *Meeting Jesus Again for the First Time: The Historical Jesus and the Heart of Contemporary Faith* (New York: HarperCollins, 1994), pp. 49-58.

2. Maya Angelou, *On the Pulse of Morning* (New York: Random House, 1993).

3. Annie Dillard, *Teaching a Stone to Talk* (New York: Harper & Row, 1982), pp. 24-26.

4. Toni Morrison, *Beloved* (New York: NAL Penguin, 1987), pp. 88-89.

Ordinary Time 23 or Proper 18

Felicia Y. Thomas

Jeremiah 18:1-11: Jeremiah speaks the word of the Lord: as a potter creates and destroys vessels of clay, so God can do with Israel.

Psalm 139:1-6, 13-18: "I praise you, for I am fearfully and wonderfully made. Wonderful are your works; that I know very well."

Philemon 1-21: Paul pleads with Philemon to welcome the slave Onesimus as his brother in Christ.

Luke 14:25-33: Jesus warns that to follow him will involve great cost: "Whoever does not carry the cross and follow me cannot be my disciple."

REFLECTIONS

When preaching the lectionary, I begin preparation by reading the passages again and again, looking either for the common thread that binds the lessons together or for the passage that grabs me. Sometimes I settle on the lesson that resonates and encourages, in short, the passage to which I most easily relate. At other times I am drawn to the difficult word—the word that challenges and confounds.

Psalm 139 hits me from every angle. It is a familiar psalm, one that I have read hundreds of times. It touches me in a deep, personal place: "Lord, you have searched me and known me." It speaks comfort and reassurance: "I come to the end—I am still with you." It perplexes: "Such knowledge is too wonderful for me." It demands: "How weighty to me are your thoughts, O God!" It speaks eloquently but not glibly or hastily. It is abstract and complex—full of powerful images, strong cadences, and graceful language.

I read and listened to this Psalm very carefully, only to discover that its themes of divine knowledge and self-discovery are simpler to read than to preach. At one level, this psalm is straightforward in its content. Yet there is also mystery and irony here. Yes, God knows each individual fully and intimately, but we are not able to fathom the real depth of such knowledge, nor its wide-ranging implications. The full weight and meaning of such knowledge eludes us because we are not able to know anyone or anything as well as God does. Still, this psalm invites us into a process of deeper spiritual awareness and greater self-discovery.

A SERMON BRIEF

One of my seminary professors once suggested that if I read Psalm 139 everyday for a year it would transform my spiritual life in a remarkable way. So I took him up on his suggestion. I diligently read it for an extended period of time, and it became a basis for developing deeper spiritual devotion and positive self-esteem.

The awareness of God's searching and knowing overwhelms me. I approached this psalm like a child who initiates a game of hide and seek. We all know the game: one person closes her eyes and counts to ten, while the other playmates hide. When the count has ended, the search begins.

My three-year-old son loves to hide, and he laughs with glee each time I find him, scoop him into my arms, and tickle his ribs with abandon. He can play this game endlessly, day in and day out. The game would not be much fun if I failed to seek him out or if I was unable to find him, for then he might be lost. Few things are more frightening to a child than the experience of being lost.

Children are not the only ones who play hide and seek. We adults play, too, but we are more sophisticated players. We no longer hide physically, but emotionally and spiritually. We take great pains to conceal our true motives, desires, and feelings from others, those closest to us, and even God. It is a game we cannot win. In being sought out, we fear exposure. In being found out, we fear abandonment. If no one acts to seek or find us, we are subject to anxiety and insecurity, and run the risk of being hopelessly lost. We harbor within a childlike terror of being lost and cut off from all that is nurturing, safe, and secure.

Our hiding reflects our longing to be sought after and to be found. And therein lies the dilemma. We want to be known and loved for

151

who we really are, but we fear that no one who really knows will truly love us.

But God sees and knows our moves, motives, thoughts, and processes. God is not repulsed by the knowing, but seeks us out and finds us so that we will not be lost. God's providential care surrounds us—guiding, protecting, instructing, encouraging. God's creative will and power forms and re-forms us, from womb to tomb. Its force enables us to become what God desires us to be: whole, loving, gracious, and just.

By God's power we are able to affirm ourselves as more than the sum total of our limits and failures. Instead we see the possibility and the hope that is present in each of us. We can claim the wonder and awesomeness of who we are—not out of conceit or grossly inflated egos, but in praise of God's handiwork, which we surely are. As we submit to God's perusal, we come to see ourselves more clearly and in so doing, to see others as fearfully and wonderfully made, too.

God's eye is on each of us. God's love surrounds us. It is trustworthy. Faithful. Powerful. Transformative. Liberating. God's love is real because it is not based on illusion or farce. It is grounded in knowing. The seeing and knowing of ourselves and others through being seen and known by God is the answer to the insecurity, fear, and anxiety that run rampant in this age. Accepting and loving ourselves and others, as a result of being loved and loving God, is the antidote to poor self-esteem, despair, and strife.

God invites our seeking and knowing, despite the limits of our best efforts. As we desire earnestly to know God's will and to do it, God reveals Godself to us. God increases our awareness of the power of God's love. God's power opens our hearts to receive God's love, acceptance, pardon, and redemption. There is no need to hide from God. And let's face it; trying to hide from our creator is an exercise in futility. Our time and energy are better spent seeking God's presence within ourselves and one another, and celebrating each new discovery.

SUGGESTIONS FOR WORSHIP

Call to Worship (in unison)

I praise you, God, for you are fearful and wonderful.
I praise you, God, for I am fearful and wonderful.
We praise you, God, for we are fearful and wonderful.
We praise you, God, for all things fearfully and wonderfully made.

Prayer of Confession (in unison)

Merciful, loving God, you see us as we really are and know us better than we know ourselves. We confess the futility of our efforts to hide from ourselves and from you. Forgive us for every thought, word, and act that is offensive in your sight. Grant us, we pray, eyes and hearts to see the wonder in ourselves and in all your creation, that we might live with justice and compassion, through Jesus Christ, our Lord. Amen.

Assurance of Pardon

Since we are God's people, created in God's image, and precious in God's sight, let us live to God's glory, affirming God's presence among us and within us. Amen.

Benediction

Lord, please look on us with grace;
watch over us with love;
and surround us with peace. Amen.

Contributors

Barbara Berry-Bailey, formerly a public broadcasting executive, serves as pastor of Trinity Lutheran Church in the Germantown section of Philadelphia, Pennsylvania. A regular contributor to several Lutheran publications, she is married to John Baily, and mother to Cynthia Bailey and Kenneth Diggs. She is head-over-heels in love with Darren and Cynthia's daughter, Zion. However, she refuses to admit that she is a grandmother, and is on a quest for a word with less baggage than "grandma."

Kathy Black, Gerald H. Kennedy Associate Professor of Homiletics and Liturgics at the Claremont School of Theology in southern California. Kathy is the author of *A Healing Homiletic: Preaching and Disabilities, Worship Across Cultures,* and *Signs of Solidarity: Ministry with Persons who are Deaf, Deafened, and Hard of Hearing.* She is ordained in the United Methodist Church, and has a strong interest in feminist liturgy and the use of arts in worship.

Melinda Contreras-Byrd, owner and director of the Generations Center of Cherry Hill, New Jersey, a unique facility which specializes in issues of race, faith, gender, and ethnicity. Melinda is an ordained elder of the African Methodist Episcopal Church and a licensed psychologist with over twenty years of experience as a therapist and workshop leader. She has given lectures, workshops, sermons, and keynote addresses throughout the United States and Latin America, is married, and lives in Princeton, New Jersey with her two daughters, Alexa and Kamaria.

Barbara Cawthorne Crafton, rector of St. Clement's Episcopal Church in Manhattan. This struggling city parish is also an off-Broadway theater with a significant ministry to the acting community as well as those who live, work, or wander in the Times Square area. Barbara is a nationally known author, retreat leader, and speaker. An actress and director, she has founded two theater companies resident in churches, and produces, directs, and sometimes performs in New York City. She is the author of a number of books, including *The Sewing Room: Uncommon Reflections on Life, Love, and Work* and most recently, *Living Lent: Meditations for These Forty Days,* as well as articles, radio scripts, and plays.

LaVerne M. Gill, pastor of the historic Webster United Church of Christ in Dexter, Michigan. LaVerne is the author of *African American Women in Congress: Forming and Transforming History, African Biblical Women and the Virtues of Womanhood,* and *My Mother Prayed for Me: Faith Journaling for African American Women.* She is also a frequent lecturer at Princeton Theological

Seminary's School of Continuing Education. She is married to Dr. Tepper Gill, a mathematician and physicist, and is the mother of two sons, Dylan and Tepper, and two stepdaughters, Jennette and Dorian.

Sylvia C. Guinn-Ammons, Presbyterian pastor and author. The Colorado license plates on Sylvia's car read "RISKIT." This is her motto for a ministry taking her from Denver, Colorado to Moscow, Russia. Christ's Universal Church has been a constant anchor during thirty-seven moves. Presently, she is researching, writing, and overseeing the publishing of a book celebrating the thirty-fifth anniversary of the Jinishian Memorial Program, an endowment administered by the Presbyterian Church (USA) to help poor and needy Armenians in the Middle East.

Susan Henry-Crowe, Dean of the Chapel and Religious Life at Emory University in Atlanta, Georgia. Ordained a United Methodist minister in 1974, Susan served as a pastor, an administrator, and a university chaplain (at Emory) before assuming her current post. In 1995 she was awarded the Candler School of Theology Alumni/ae Award. The citation she received at the time called her "a trailblazer for ordained women, pioneering in many ways during more than two decades." While working at Emory she has been especially concerned to foster interreligious dialogue in the ever changing world of religious pluralism.

René Rodgers Jensen, copastor, First Christian Church, Omaha, Nebraska. René finds that Nebraska winters test her character and Nebraska springs restore her faith. She feels blessed to work with her husband of three decades, and as the parent of one college and one high school student is working hard on cultivating the spiritual gifts of wisdom and discernment.

Mary Emaline Kraus, pastor of the historic Dumbarton United Methodist Church in Washington, D.C. Since graduating from Boston University School of Theology in 1972, the focus of Mary's ministry has been on the local church, except for the six years that she served as a District Superintendent. Her love of preaching is matched only by the deep satisfaction of empowering laity and seminarians to find their voices in proclaiming the Word. "The best decision I ever made was to finally say 'Yes' to God's call to ministry."

Laura Loving, United Church of Christ pastor, writer, retreat leader, and student. Linda is a part-time supply pastor and travels widely as a seminar and retreat leader in areas ranging from spirituality to conflict resolution, journaling to prayer. She coauthored a book on family worship, *Celebrating at Home: Prayers and Liturgies for Families*. She lives in Wisconsin with her spouse, three children, a parakeet, and stacks of books, newspapers, videos, and magazines. When Laura is not traveling or serving the parish, she nests at home with the *New York Times* crossword puzzle, baking, reading, and learning the formidable spiritual discipline of being a spouse and a parent.

Barbara K. Lundblad, Associate Professor of Preaching at Union Theological Seminary, New York. Barbara grew up on a farm in Iowa and her roots are still there even though she had been transplanted to New York City where she

155

was pastor of Our Savior's Atonement Lutheran Church in Washington Heights for sixteen years. She loves wandering through New York neighborhoods, delighting in the wild diversity of the city. In the summer she heads north to Deer Isle, Maine, listening to the quiet and kayaking among the islands of Penobscott Bay.

Ella Pearson Mitchell is an octogenarian mother and grandmother who still team teaches with her husband as a Visiting Professor of Homiletics at the Interdenominational Theological Center in Atlanta. She has four books in print, the latest being *Together for Good,* a joint autobiography with her husband. Ella is much in demand as a preacher and lecturer across the country, and is currently copresident of the Academy of Homiletics. A graduate of Talladega College in Alabama, with a joint Masters degree from Columbia University and Union Theological Seminary, Ella holds a Doctorate of Ministry degree from Claremont School of Theology.

Karen Pidcock-Lester, copastor of the First Presbyterian Church in Pottstown, Pennsylvania, has previously served congregations in Indianapolis, Baltimore, and Richmond, Virginia. Kerry has preached at continuing education events at Union/PSCE and Princeton Seminary, and published essays in *Interpretation, Reformed Liturgy and Music,* and *God Who Creates*. Her chief delights are watching (with her husband Carter) their three daughters unfold into women, taking teenagers on work camps, belting out Broadway tunes at the piano, and talking with old friends until the candles burn low.

Janet Schlichting, O.P., Dominican Sister of Akron, Ohio. Janet has been preaching retreats and parish missions for twenty years, in addition to serving as an art teacher, liturgy coodinator, and spiritual director. She holds a D.Min. in preaching from Aquinas Institute of Theology. "What defines me as a preacher is a certain intensity or passion in wrestling the scriptures and God for a blessing, for a word of grace and truth."

Felicia Y. Thomas, pastor of First Baptist Church in Princeton, New Jersey. Felicia is the first woman to serve as pastor of this historic African American congregation. *Ebony* magazine recently named her one of the most outstanding African American preachers in the United States. In life and ministry Felicia says she is nurtured by the love and support of her husband, mother, and two young sons. She enjoys walking, reading, and visiting with friends whenever she has the opportunity.

Lynda Weaver-Williams teaches in the department of Philosophy and Religious Studies at Virginia Commonwealth University in Richmond, Virginia. In a former life, she was a Baptist pastor. In her heart of hearts she still is, finding ways to tell the Story on a secular campus and preach the Story as itinerant ministry shapes her call these days. A transplanted Texan, she credits the small town Baptist church where she grew up with teaching her how to "love to tell the Story." She is married and is the mother of two teenage sons.

Index

Subject Index

Scripture Index

160